I0101869

Cowboy Sweethearts

by

Judy Goodspeed

Dragonfly Publishing, Inc.

All rights reserved. No part of this book may be reproduced electronically, or by any form, or by any means without the prior written consent of the Publisher and the Author, except in brief quotes used in interviews or for review purposes.

COWBOY SWEETHEARTS
Paperback Edition [Non-Fiction / Biography]
EAN 978-0-9817049-9-9 | ISBN 0-9817049-9-9

Text Copyright ©2006 Judy Goodspeed
Dragonfly Logo Copyright ©2001 Terri Branson
Cover Photograph by Dudley Barker (used with permission)
Jacket design and additional illustrations by Terri Branson

Published in the United States of America by
Dragonfly Publishing, Inc. of Oklahoma

Table of Contents

Dedication

This book is dedicated to the memory of my nephew, Mark Allen King, who died in 1972 at the age of thirteen. Although cancer robbed him of a long life, it never lessened his compassion, optimism, courage, and incredible sense of humor. The illness took him in eighteen months, but his spirit can and will endure in my heart and mind forever.

Cowboy Sweethearts

Acknowledgements

So many people have helped make this book possible. First, I would like to thank Judy Dearing for giving me the idea. Next, I would like to thank the eleven wonderful women who shared their life stories and photographs with me.

Thanks to a special lady Terri Branson, my editor, who not only laughs at my internet ignorance but also encourages and teaches me. Also, thanks to Randa, Naomi, Carol, Debbie, LaNita, Brenda, Evelyn, June, Pat, and the members of my writers group for listening to me and critiquing for me. And last, thanks to my parents Buck and Decie Goodspeed for the many hours spent in an arena or at a rodeo.

Introduction

Cowboy Sweethearts is based on interviews with eleven women, whose husbands were active in professional rodeo or who were themselves active. This book tells about their lives in rodeo. Some stayed home while their husbands traveled. Most traveled with their husbands. Others were, and some still are, active participants in rodeo. The main objective in each case has been for each woman to help her husband succeed.

For Better or Worse

By Judy Goodspeed

It's three in the morning, I'm packing your bag.
Don't want you to leave, but know not to nag.
Just married a week and now you must go
With Everett and Dick to the Denver rodeo.

For better of worse, that's what we said
But nobody mentioned this half-empty bed.

Two years of marriage, a son on the way
Time for the hospital but you can't stay.
You're leading the average tonight at Fort Worth.
So you have to miss your first baby's birth.

For better or worse, that's what we said
But nobody mentioned this half-empty bed.

The cows are out. Cody has colic.
If I drank I'd be an alcoholic.
The phone rings, you're coming home.
Two wonderful days and then you're gone.

For better or worse that's what we said
But nobody mentioned this half-empty bed.

The days are too short, the nights are too long.
I cry every time I hear a sad song.
Don't know how much loneliness I can take.
Perhaps this marriage is a total mistake.

For better or worse, that's what we said
But nobody mentioned this half-empty bed.

Just when I decide I've had enough.
That the life of a rodeo wife is too tough.
You walk through the door as handsome as sin,
Open your arms, grin that lopsided grin.
And that's when better starts over again.

I

Vicki
Herrera Adams

WHEN she was asked to perform her specialty act at the prestigious *Budweiser World Cup* in Las Vegas, Nevada, Vicki felt honored.

This competition, held in the Thomas and Mack Arena, featured the elite jumping horses of the world. Vicki and her horse Butterfly were to perform, while the jumps were removed to ready the arena for the next round of competition. Little did she know that this performance would be a great test of her training and mental skills.

Before the performance, Vicki and Butterfly were not allowed to use the warm up areas designated for the million-dollar jumpers, so they found another area. While they were warming up, Butterfly stepped on a rock and suffered a stone bruise. He was limping when Vicki rode to the arena.

"I don't think he can do it," Vicki had told her husband Leon.

"He'll forget about it when he gets in there," Leon had replied.

"The show must go on."

"When I rode into the arena it was a total black house except for the spotlight on me," Vicki recalled. "I was in there performing while they were taking down the elaborate jumps. When the spotlight hit one, my horse looked at it and I had to keep a tight leg on him to direct him here and there. I was going through jumps, I was going through ferns, and I was going through helpers hauling out poles on their shoulders. You talk about pressure. There isn't a horse in the world that should be put into that condition and work. He listened to everything I said."

Butterfly performed magnificently, despite the bruise, which later abscessed and had to be treated. He could not perform for a couple of weeks afterward, but did fully recover.

Vicki Herrera dreamed of being a rodeo performer from an early age greatly due to the influence of Bill Herrera, her father, who was All Around Rodeo Champion in the Northwest Indian Rodeo Association. He began working with Vicki when she was very young and was instrumental in her success as a trick rider and barrel racer.

The Herrera family lived on the Yakama Indian Reservation near Toppenish, Washington. Bill and Gladys Herrera had three children: Vicki, Susan Claire (nicknamed "Bobbi" because Vicki couldn't pronounce "baby"), and son Billy. Bill Herrera worked in construction and on his wife's uncle's ranch, when he was not gone to a rodeo. He was a skilled horseman, marksman, and trapper.

"We never ate beef or pork," Vicki recalled. "Dad provided us with all kinds of wild game. I hunted ducks and pheasant with him, but didn't enjoy hunting much. I guess I was a pretty good shot, because when I was sixteen I won a turkey shoot. Dad entered the competition, and I was just along to watch. When he found out they were having a women's competition, he entered me."

Vicki wasn't happy about him entering her, because she didn't have her twenty-gauge shotgun and she certainly wasn't dressed like the other contestants. The other women had on hunting gear complete with fancy vests with all of the little loops filled with shells.

"Dad said, 'You can use my twelve-gauge,' as he handed me the heavy shotgun," Vicki recalled.

Knowing it was useless to protest, Vicki lined up with the other women and the competition began. The first time she shot the gun, the recoil almost spun her in a complete circle. Her shoulder felt like it had been torn off, but she busted her skeet and prepared to shoot again.

"I flinched every time I shot, but I kept on hitting my skeet. Finally, there was only one other woman and me left. I don't remember even seeing the skeet, but somehow I hit it and won the match. My shoulder was bruised and sore for days."

Vicki went with her dad everywhere and doesn't remember when she started riding horses. It was quite a shock when she realized that she had to go to school. She didn't like the idea of being confined five days a week. She didn't want to be there and couldn't seem to stay focused on her work. A slight speech problem made her shy and uncomfortable. Speech therapy and an understanding school principal helped her get through those difficult first years.

"My principal was a bull rider, so he knew how my mind worked. He was very kind."

She wasn't very social, preferring to have one friend at a time. Although Vicki would go home with her friend, she never invited anyone home with her. The Herreras' house wasn't modern. Mrs. Herrera heated water and poured it into a galvanized tub for the family to bathe. The toilet was an outhouse.

Vicki's grandparents lived within walking distance. Her grandfather was the tribal game warden and a tribal policeman. Her grandmother was a tribal judge. They had a nice modern house that Vicki enjoyed very much.

"I spent a lot of time with my grandparents. Sometimes it got a little chaotic at my house, so I would go to Grandmother's where I felt secure. She cooked fry bread and baked all sorts of things."

Vicki's great-grandmother was another source of comfort and knowledge. A full-blood Cowlitz, the elderly woman loved to camp in the mountains and tell stories about the old ways.

"She always had her coffeepot and all the fixings in a cardboard box ready in case someone came along and would take her camping. We picked huckleberries in beautiful handmade baskets and camped on Potato Mountain. At night, we sat around the campfire and listened to stories. Those were wonderful times."

When she wasn't at school or out camping, Vicki rode horses and helped her dad with the livestock. She had a little buckskin mare that she rode up and down the drain ditch and the roads. The year she was eleven she received a trick riding saddle for Christmas, and her father began to train her as best he could.

"When I was eleven we were at a rodeo in Oregon," Vicki recalled. "I saw a trick rider perform there. I remember her screaming and falling off to the side of her horse. The scream got my attention because I was playing and not really watching. She screamed and fell into a Russian Cossack drag. Wow, that's pretty interesting. I can do that, I thought."

From age eleven to age fifteen Vicki barrel raced and practiced trick riding. Her mother trained a little brown King-bred horse for her. Vicki named the horse King. The well-matched pair won the barrel racing championship in the Northwest Indian Rodeo Association for four years.

She was sixteen when she came across trick riders, Dick and Connie Griffith, at a rodeo at Ellensberg, Washington. After the couple performed, Vicki followed them back to camp and more or less had an interview with Dick. He asked many questions, turned her all around and looked her over to see if she was physically fit. Since they were going to be in Ellensberg for a couple of weeks Dick agreed to train Vicki, if she would come up after school.

"I barely had my license, but I loaded my mare and drove up everyday after school to have a lesson with him," Vicki said. "I remember my hands were just blistered from gripping the saddle horn. He would take raw tape and wrap around my thumbs and palms, but I was determined and hung in there."

She was such a good student that Dick and Connie asked her to stay with them and continue her training. It was a great opportunity. Vicki went with them to California, attended school and practiced trick riding. This training was the beginning of a career in trick riding where she worked with some of the best in the business.

In 1968 Vicki trick rode with Connie Griffith, Jimmy Maderas, and Candy Rodewald at the Cow Palace in San Francisco, California. Later that same year at Puyallup, Washington, she met and practiced with Dick and Beth Hammond, an older married trick riding couple. Connie Griffith also performed at Puyallup.

In 1969 the Yakama Nation asked Vicki to represent them in the *Miss Indian America Pageant*. She agreed to enter the pageant and began a crash course in Native American dance, tribal economics and politics, and how to wear her feather properly. Although many of her cousins were dancers and had entered dance competition, Vicki was busy with her rodeo career and had never learned to dance. She did learn, and with her great-grandmother accompanying her, she traveled to Sheridan, Wyoming where the pageant was held. There were fifty tribes represented. The first *Miss Indian America* was Mrs. Herrera's cousin, Gladys James. No Yakama had placed since that first contest.

"I think where I messed up was when they asked me the interview question," Vicki said. "The question was: 'You know if you win you have to live with a strange family for a whole year in Sheridan, and you have to represent your people at different functions; are you willing to do that?'"

Vicki stammered and stuttered, thinking: *What about my trick riding? What about my rodeo? What about my horses?*

"I told them I wouldn't be here if I didn't want to be," Vicki added. "But I don't think they believed me, so I was an alternate. I think I could have done a lot better, even won it if I hadn't hesitated on the interview question. My heart wasn't in it, because I really didn't live the traditional Indian way. I was into my cows and horses. That's what I wanted to do."

After graduation from high school, Vicki decided to go professional. She joined the RCA (Rodeo Cowboys' Association), known today as the PRCA (Professional Rodeo Cowboys' Association), and booked several rodeos for the following summer.

Her little sister, Bobbi, had begun trick riding also and they had perfected a show together. However, the act did not happen because at The Contract Act Convention in Denver, Colorado, Vicki met Leon Adams, a cowboy from Oklahoma.

Leon, along with competing in rodeo events, had the only specialty act of its kind in the world. This act featured Leon Roman riding his well-trained Brahma bulls, Geronimo and Apache. Later he added an act called *The Flying Aces*, which included him Roman riding horses then doing a shoulder stand between the fast running magnificent animals.

"I guess Leon took a liking to me because he invited me to

come to Oklahoma with him and learn to Roman ride," Vick said. "I came down that spring and lived with his sister and brother-in-law. I went out to the ranch and began trick riding and Roman riding his horses. One thing led to the next. Six months later, he decided we should get married. He didn't want me to go back to the Northwest."

She did return home and prepared to honor the contracts she had made earlier that year. Leon was at a rodeo in California. He called her at her grandmother's and asked her to marry him. She said yes. He had his horses with him, so between shows he borrowed a Cadillac from a friend and drove to Washington. He picked up Vicki, Bobbi, and their horses and took them to a rodeo in Redding, California, where they were to perform. They also performed at Santa Maria, California.

Leon and Vicki got married at Santa Maria in June of 1970. The next weekend at Livermore, Vicki's parents came to get Bobbi and the horses. Vicki's dad wanted to take her home with them. Once they convinced her father they were actually married, Vicki and Leon returned to Oklahoma.

"I had to get someone to take my place at the rodeos I had scheduled. Penny Lyons agreed to ride for me with Bobbi."

This was the first time Vicki had ever gone against her father's wishes. All of her life he had protected her. He didn't allow her to participate in extracurricular activities, because he didn't want her away from home in the evening. She only attended one prom and it was at another school. Her date was a calf roper that her father knew and they doubled dated with her cousin, otherwise she wouldn't have been allowed to go.

Every year a high school livestock show was held at the stockyards in Toppenish, Washington. It was common for junior and seniors to skip school and go to the show. No one ever got into trouble, since most of the kids were there showing animals. One year Vicki and her friend decided to skip school and go to the show. They were walking with a group of students toward the show barn, when she saw her dad come out of the sale barn.

"There's my dad," Vicki said. The other kids scattered like quail, leaving Vicki and her friend standing there. Then for some reason, they ran, too. "Well, he saw us and followed us to another friend's house. He marched right into the house and told us to come out. He knew we were there. We came out of the closet. Dad took us back to school and had a few words with the principal. I never skipped school again."

Needless to say, Mr. Herrera wasn't happy about his daughter marrying a cowboy from Oklahoma. He took her horses and wouldn't give them back. All she could take with her was her trick riding saddle she had received for Christmas when she was eleven years old.

"I had to start over, but Leon assured me that he would help me train another trick riding horse," Vicki said. "While we were working on my act, I learned to Roman ride and assist Leon in setting up props for his acts. He was a perfectionist, but later when he pulled a hamstring I had to take over the *Flying Aces*. I rode them a couple of seasons. We also had a double team act, and later a six up tandem style. I went to performing One Little Indian, a black and white stallion, in a very unique dancing and trick horse routine. The hind leg walk was his specialty. So special that we won the Specialty Act of the Year in 1984."

The couple drove from rodeo to rodeo, pulling their trailer behind a van full of animals. Vicki hated the truck they drove, because it broke down all the time. Sometimes they made it to a rodeo just in time to unload their horses, throw on their costumes and dash into the arena. She was greatly relieved when they made enough money to buy a new rig.

During the time that Leon was recovering from his hamstring injury, Vicki performed the Roman riding act in his place. When he was ready to ride again, they decided to add Vicki and another team to the act. They rode on two pairs of horses, and then switched teams while flying around the arena. What began as a temporary job lasted for six years.

"We were performing at Jackson, Mississippi, and I got upset with Leon for being over protective," Vicki said. "I told him just to worry about his part of the deal. The next performance he, more or less, ignored me. When we started to switch teams, he handed me the reins and didn't even look at me. I knew I was in trouble when I got on a tilt. All he had to do was hold out his arm, but he still didn't look at me. I fell between the teams and got clipped in the ribs by a flying hoof. I was sore for a few days, and a little less verbal."

In l975 Vicki had spotted a little paint horse that came from the Osage Indian Reservation. She and her father-in-law approached the owner of the black and white paint and bought him. She named him One Little Indian. Horse trainer and showman Glen Randall trained One Little Indian and Vicki in dressage and marching.

"This was new to me, but I absorbed all that he presented to me. And when I left I was able to continue what Glen taught me. With Leon's help, we came up with a dance and marching act that was really special. Glen's wife, Lynn, called One Little Indian a 'rat' because he was small, but I didn't care. She probably changed her mind about the rat when he won Specialty Act of the Year in 1984."

Leon and Vicki quickly became recognized as one of the best contract acts in the business. They have been nominated twenty times for the PRCA "Contract Act of the Year" and have won the honor of "Specialty Acts of the Year" four times.

Vicki and her superbly trained horses, Silverado, Cherokee Smoke, Butterfly, Rudy, Indian Two, and Indian Three (Skipper) have presented the American Flag from 1991-2002 and again in 2004 at the National Finals Rodeo. She was asked to present again in 2005 but declined. Not only has she presented the American Flag at the Finals, but she also performed with her famous dancing horses there in 1985, 1992, 1993, 1995, 1997, and 1999.

In their thirty-five years of marriage Vicki and Leon have driven all over the United States pulling up to six horses, two Brahma bulls, and a trailer that served as their home away from home. Sometimes it was necessary for them to drive all night to reach the next show. Thirty-five years without a serious accident is quite a record. The only real problems Vicki remembers are trips from Regina, Sasakatchewan, Canada to Las Vegas, Nevada. They drove a thousand miles on ice and snow. Another trip they took a shortcut through one of the passes between Sheridan and Cody, Wyoming. They managed to pull six horses up one steep grade by gearing down to first gear. On the way down, they dealt with a ten percent grade for twelve miles.

"We got about halfway down, and when Leon hit the brakes it was just mush," Vicki said. "One side was mountain. The other side was a thousand feet down with a creek at the bottom. Our brakes locked up and we were fixing to hit the mountain. Leon was hollering: 'Bail out! Bail out!' I wouldn't do it. Everything came to a screeching halt, and we got out all shaky and weak-kneed. We went back to check the stock, and the hubs on the wheels had gotten so hot that they popped off. The wheel wells caught fire. We were running around bumping into each other trying to find the fire extinguisher. We finally found it and put out the fire. Then we unloaded the stock and got on the phone to the rodeo commissioner, and she called the sheriff."

The rodeo committee picked up the horses. Then they helped get the truck and trailer down the mountain. Many vehicles hadn't been so fortunate, going over the rim into the steep canyon.

"I asked Leon why he wasn't praying, because I was praying out loud," she recalled. "He said, 'I was too busy trying to keep this thing on the road.'"

Leon and Vicki traveled not only all over the United States, Mexico, and Canada, but also over seas. In 1989 Jerome Robinson approached Leon and Vicki with the idea of a wild-west show. They liked the plan and began to gather personnel and animals to make it happen. On one of their first trips, they took forty-seven horses. Jerome brought the horses to the Adams' ranch were they were quarantined and trained. That year they trained eight trick riding horses, three Roman riding teams, several chuck wagons teams. Several performers and trainers stayed at the ranch until the training was complete and they were ready to leave.

"That's a lot of fun having everybody around working from daylight to dark," Vicki said. "One of the trick riders, an Indian girl named Ruth Bitsui, traveled with the show to Finland and France. When she wasn't trick riding, she performed traditional dance with her husband and son. Ruth just came right in and helped with the cooking and cleaning. We had to feed everybody. We always had breakfast here, because we wanted to have at least one good meal a day. The bunkhouse, barn, and extra rooms in the house were full. We didn't want anyone going off to a motel, because they needed to be here first thing in the morning to get started. They needed to go to bed early and not go off and get in trouble. We kept everyone on the ranch and had lots of fun."

Horses and people all flew to their destination except when they went to Finland. On that trip the livestock, accompanied by a veterinarian and some of the hands, flew to Newfoundland and then on to Helsinki. The cowboys and cowgirls flew to Stockholm, Sweden, and then took a cruise ship to Helsinki.

They arrived ten days early to set up for the show. After two performances a day for four days, the horses were sold except for the six horses that Vicki and Leon owned. *The Flying Aces* team and Vicki's dancing horses returned home to Oklahoma.

The show in Japan was different. It lasted about a week and was held below Mt. Aso, an active volcano.

Most of the time, Jerome Robinson provided the livestock for the show. One exception was in Paris, France, where the French insisted on furnishing the steers for the steer wrestling competition. The problem with that arrangement was that the steers chased the cowboys after they let them up. The cowboys quickly learned to have a bullfighter on standby before they released the steer. Vicki enjoyed the trips overseas, the wild-west show, and rodeos they presented to foreign audiences.

In all of the years of traveling, the only time Vicki stayed home was when their daughter, Kerri, was born in 1974. Mrs. Herrera came for the birth of the baby and to help until Vicki recovered. When Kerri was three weeks old, she became a traveler, too.

Sometimes, when the weather was pretty or there weren't trailer hook-up facilities, they would camp out. They especially liked to camp in Colorado because of the beautiful scenery. Pine Ridge and Rosebud, South Dakota, didn't have any facilities so they camped on the rodeo grounds. This was great fun because the Sioux Indians held a Pow-Wow during the night. They would go watch the dancing and enjoy the celebration.

Like her parents, Kerri became a rodeo performer. She stayed with Leon's sister and brother-in-law during the school year and joined her parents in the summer. Kerri graduated from college with a teaching degree and taught in the public school system for five years. She and her family live on the ranch near her parents, and Kerri works for the Choctaw Nation in the GED Educational Program. Kerri has one son, Zayne, who is a rodeo contestant and the apple of his grandparents' eyes.

Vicki and Leon have reached the time in their lives when travel and performing isn't as much fun as it once was. They enjoy spending time at their ranch and being close to their family.

Vicki has attained about every goal she dreamed of as a young girl. A world renowned trick rider, she is widely acclaimed as one of the few to go from a back bend to a liberty stand and do it beautifully. Vicki is also known for doing lots of groundwork in her trick riding performances, which is one of the reasons she was chosen to perform in the documentary honoring world famous saddle maker, Monroe Veach. That documentary is now in the Smithsonian Institute.

Added to her long list of accomplishments is performing and stunt riding in the movie *Buffalo Girls*.

"I just kinda was in the background doing tricks and filling in. We furnished many of the horses for the movie. It was fun to work with Reba McEntire. She got her start in rodeo, and we've watched her since she was a teenager."

Vicki's horses are almost as famous as their trainer. Cherokee Smoke made a movie known as *Horse Crazy* and was nominated for "Specialty Act of the Year" in 2001. Six of her horses have carried Vicki and the American Flag at National Finals Rodeos. Silverado received the Versatility award at the AQHA Champion Show in 1998. He was also on the cover of *American's Horse* magazine.

One of her most treasured memories is performing with trick roper and showman, Jerry Diaz, at Denver, Colorado. While the rodeo was held in one coliseum, specialty acts were performed in another. An act of Leon's was going on in one arena while Vicki was performing in another. Then she dashed from that arena to perform with Jerry.

"It was fun and exciting to do something different," Vicki said. "I really enjoyed working with Jerry. He is so good."

In 2005, Vicki became the second woman and the first Native American woman to be inducted into the National Cowboy of Color Museum and Hall of Fame. That same year she became a nominee for the National Cowgirl Museum and Hall of Fame in Fort Worth, Texas, and she was on the ballot for the National Cowboy Hall of Fame in Oklahoma City, Oklahoma.

All wasn't always great and happy. In the spring of 1985, One Little Indian, Vicki's favorite horse, ruptured an intestine and died at Colorado Springs, Colorado. Indian Two, who was One Little Indian's brother, had to perform when he was only three and just green broke. The audience never knew she switched horses.

"I told Leon I can't do this," Vicki said. "He replied, 'The show must go on.' I had to perform like nothing had happened."

There was another time when Leon lost a horse from his Roman riding team. His brother-in-law brought a horse out of the pasture for Leon to ride.

The beautiful dapple-gray quarter horse, Silverado, was twenty-two years old when he died from a brain tumor. He and Vicki had performed together for sixteen years.

Only once did one of her horses pull something stupid. This happened at Salinas, California. About 10,000 people lined the track where Vicki and Indian Two were to entertain them.

"I'd just bragged to Leon how sweet he was and I'd like my grandchildren to have him," Vicki recalled. "I warmed him up and had to gallop quite a distance to get to my spot. I felt him tense up when he saw the people so close. He wanted to play. Then he planted his feet, and I did a 360 over his head and landed on my butt right under his nose. I was wearing a feathered costume and was concerned about any damage that might have been done, plus I was embarrassed at being dumped. Thank heavens he didn't run off. He stood looking at me. Leon came out to help me get back together. I asked him if my feathers were broken. He replied, 'You look like you've been in a chicken fight.' I told him to shut up and just get me through this! I had to get on and do my routine. I was so embarrassed. My friend, the announcer could hardly compose himself, because he saw Leon smiling. The next week the announcer got dumped in an introduction. He shouldn't have laughed at me."

As a youngster, Vicki asked for help and guidance from the Lord so that she might live her dream. That guidance began with her parents. Bill Herrera gave her instruction in trick riding and horsemanship, and her mother trained her first barrel horse and sewed her clothes for her. Looking back, Vicki realizes that if her father hadn't been so over protective she probably would have gotten into trouble. She also realized that if she hadn't gone against his wishes she wouldn't have accomplished all she did.

She feels that opportunities came to her like stepping-stones, training with the Griffiths, meeting Leon, training with Glen Randall, and performing with the best in the world.

Vicki loved Leon enough to say "no" to her father whom she

had never before disobeyed. Her mother was concerned about their age difference, but didn't try to stop the marriage.

"I know that I made my mother sad. Having a daughter of my own helped me to realize what my mother went through when I left. I can't imagine Kerri leaving here and moving to Washington."

Leon says that he's the luckiest man in the world, and Vicki says that he is her partner, mentor, and best friend. They must have something very special to have spent twenty-four hours a day together for thirty-five years.

"We sometimes would grumble and gripe at each other during an act, but the audience never knew it," Vicki said. "Basically, we have always worked well together and had lots of fun. I wasn't going to stay home and let him go on the road without me. Too many things can happen to a marriage if couples are apart. I even went with Leon and Marty Melvin when they went off to steer wrestle. Leon hazed for Marty and then Marty hazed for him. Leon helped Marty make it to the Southwest NFR about six times. Marty came in second one of those years. Leon used my barrel horse to haze on. We had two teams to make it to the NFR in one year. So it was worth while hauling them when we weren't showing."

Vicki hazed for Leon in the practice pen at home and back east where hazers were scarce. If he was unsure about the situation, he asked Vicki to haze for him.

Although she didn't win the Miss Indian America title, Vicki represented her people and women all over the world for many years. She pursued her dream and accomplished it through good choices and hard work.

As of 2006, she continued to make a few shows a year, but spent most of her time on the ranch. She did remark that her son-in-law was into archery competition, which was something she might like to try next.

Vicki Adams Roman riding a pair of paint horses through a hoop of fire.

Vicki Adams with bowing paints, as she salutes the
audience at the end of a performance.

Vicki Adams doing the back bend at a rodeo in Iowa.

Vicki Adams (in tail drag) with sister Bobbi (standing) during a performance in Oregon (1966).

Vicki Adams performing her specialty act with her horse, One Little Indian.

Leon Adams performing his unique Roman riding act with Brahma bulls, Geronimo and Apache.

Vicki Herrera Adams

Leon Adams with grandson Zayne at their ranch in
Stuart, Okahoma (2005).

Leon and Vicki Adams posing between performances (date and location unknown).

II

Margaret
Hart Deakins

WHEN her only child left home to attend college at Oklahoma State University, and her husband, Ab, was away at work, Margaret was lost.

The empty nest syndrome propelled her into seeking ways to keep busy. She thought her situation over and decided that her basic skills were cleaning and organizing. A housecleaning business just might be the ticket.

Two of her friends liked Margaret's plan. One put up the operating money, another agreed to keep books, and Margaret was in charge of buying supplies and equipment. The *Occasional Thorough Housecleaning Service* was ready for business.

"I ran an ad in the paper but it was a long time before anyone called," Margaret said. "I went to a lady's house and gave her an estimate which she accepted. Now I needed a crew. Again friends came to mind and I hired four ladies that I knew were honest and reliable."

At first Margaret helped with the cleaning, but after her crew became experienced she mostly supervised and did estimates.

"Everything in a room was moved and cleaned behind," she explained. "The only thing we didn't do was the outside of windows. It usually took more than one day to finish a house. I made sure that I didn't agree to do houses that were really bad. You wouldn't believe some of the places that I visited. Walls were all marked up and damaged--that sort of thing. Those kinds of houses would take several days and still wouldn't look any better."

Over the years, the other partners dropped out and Margaret became sole owner of the company. Business was good, and many times they had two jobs going at the same time. Margaret was helping her crew when she accidentally discovered a new service.

"One client had a large stuffed chair that was in terrible shape. The cushions were all mashed down and the chair needed a good cleaning. I asked one of the girls to help me. We covered the chair with a plastic bag and sucked the dirt out with a vacuum. I fluffed the cushions, rearranged the furniture and did a picture grouping. My helper was worried that the lady would be upset, but she wasn't," Margaret added. "She loved the arrangement and couldn't believe how good the chair looked. That prompted me to take an interior decorating class."

She enjoyed doing picture groupings and rearranging, but didn't get overly involved in decorating. Thinking it might be fun and profitable, Margaret went to work for an interior decorating company. However, she didn't enjoy it, and quit to concentrate on her cleaning business. Many of her customers became friends and Margaret kept in contact with them after she retired.

"We had a country house that we cleaned for an elderly couple. The gentleman loved for us to come and insisted that I let the girls clean so that I was free to go for a walk with him or help feed the ducks. He went to great lengths cooking for us and serving lunch on the patio. We all looked forward to going to their house," Margaret said.

Three or four days a week Margaret supervised her crew, bought supplies, and gave estimates on possible jobs. She also served as vice-president of the Democratic Party in Del City. Weekends were spent driving her husband Ab to rodeos, or attending rodeos where Ab junior was performing.

When good help became hard to find, Margaret gave up her business. She did picture grouping and decorating part-time but finally retired completely.

Margaret Hart was born and raised near Shawnee, Oklahoma. Her father was a farmer, but also hired out to local lumber companies hauling lumber to building sites. Margaret was next to the youngest in a family of six sons and five daughters.

The family lived in a long ranch style house with a large screened in porch on one side. The boys slept on the porch. In the winter, shutters covered the windows and a large wood stove helped keep the porch warm.

"I think almost every room in the house had a wood stove in it," Margaret recalled. "The one in the kitchen was huge and had a water reservoir on one side. We always had hot water for dish washing and for bathing."

The dining table was ten to twelve feet long with wooden benches on each side. Mr. Hart sat at one end, Mrs. Hart sat at the other end, and the children sat on the benches.

"We never went without necessities," Margaret said. "I suppose we were poor, but I never thought much about it. I do remember Mother washing in a big black pot out in the yard. That was a hard job that required lots of water hauling."

There were many things for kids to do. Margaret and her brothers played in the sand along the creek most of the time. They found discarded beer bottles and pretended that they were horses. The boys taught her how to make harnesses out of scrap leather and to make wagons out of cigar boxes.

When Mr. Hart brought home a paint horse, riding became a favorite activity. Margaret's brother Joe decided to become a trick rider. He worked at odd jobs and saved until he had enough money to buy an old trick riding saddle. He began practicing. Margaret tried a few tricks, but quickly decided that trick riding was not her thing. She did, however, love to ride.

They rode bareback most of the time and climbed one of the many cherry trees to mount their horse. Visiting an older brother was a favorite past time. He and his wife lived down the road a few miles. Many times Margaret and Joe would ride down for a visit but find their mount missing when it was time to leave. The horse was good at getting loose and returning home.

"After we walked home a few times, we learned to tie him better," Margaret recalled.

Another favorite activity was swimming in a water hole under a railroad trestle. There were large rocks all around the water and the sides were steep. One afternoon one of Margaret's friends encouraged her to dive. Climbing up the steep side Margaret's foot slipped and she cut herself on a sharp rock.

"I was bleeding all over the place and scared to death," Margaret said. "Thank goodness there were several kids with me and they managed to get me to the house. Dad looked at my foot and then left the house. He came back in a little bit with some cow manure. I about fainted when he put the manure on the cut and wrapped it up. I had to sleep outside that night because I smelled so bad. The cut didn't swell or give me any trouble."

Margaret attended Shawnee Public Schools most of her early years. The only exception was the year she attended St. Benedict's Catholic School. She wasn't Catholic but her best friend was, so the family arranged for Margaret to live with them and go to school with their daughter.

"I babysat and cared for an elderly lady to pay my tuition. It was a good experience. When my friend moved away, I went back to public school."

Margaret's older sister, Lela, was a businesswoman. Lela's husband was often away on business trips. She wanted something to do, so he bought her a cattle truck. Lela attended livestock auctions and hauled cattle for buyers. Margaret sometimes went with her. On one of these trips, Margaret met her future husband.

Ab Deakins was a cattle buyer from Oklahoma City and often attended the sale at Shawnee. He bought a load of cattle and hired Lela to haul them to the City for him. Margaret went with Lela to deliver the cattle and met Ab. They visited and she told him she liked horses.

"Next thing you know, here comes Ab with an old mare for me to ride," Margaret said. "Well, that was fine with me. My sister-in-law loved to ride, too, so we rode almost everyday. When we discovered a riding academy in Shawnee, we picked cotton in the mornings so we could ride at the academy in the afternoon. I think it cost fifty cents an hour to ride. We also joined the local Roundup Club and had a lot of fun riding in parades and rodeos."

Lela continued hauling cattle for Ab, and Margaret went with her. Ab began to visit Margaret in Shawnee. After dating about a year, Ab proposed and the couple became engaged.

"We both loved horses and cattle, so we got along well. We were engaged for three years. I visited Ab in Oklahoma City at his parents' on weekends and we went to rodeos. Ab loved to rope and I loved to go with him."

The couple married in 1942 and moved in with Ab's mother, who was then living alone.

"She wouldn't let me do anything but clean house and wash dishes. I couldn't even cook dinner for my husband. I was not happy with the arrangement and talked to Ab about moving."

Ab's office was at the Stockyards in Oklahoma City, so he found them an apartment in that area. Margaret was much happier even though it meant driving back to his mother's everyday to feed the livestock. When Ab was away buying cattle Margaret took care of the feeding for him.

Business grew and Ab was away much of the time. One of his business ventures was buying and selling roping calves. These calves were purchased by cowboys to practice roping and by local stock contractors to use in rodeos. Ab traveled to Texas, Kansas, and Florida buying calves. He usually kept one to two hundred calves at the home pasture. The chore of feeding and showing them soon became Margaret's job.

"I would meet the buyer and he would pick out the calves he wanted. Then we would sort them out, haggle over prices, and load them. I took care of all the cattle at home and kept the books. We bought and sold calves for several years."

Ab liked for Margaret to go with him on trips out of state. She couldn't figure out why, because they took two cattle trucks and Margaret rode with one driver and Ab rode with the other. They made many trips to Texas and Kansas.

Feeling that it was time to start a family and find a place with a few acres, Margaret and Ab started looking for houses. They found a house and a few acres in Oklahoma City and bought it. Margaret still lives in that house.

Weekends were spent at rodeos. Ab roped calves and steers. He wasn't a world champion, but he was a good roper. Margaret did the driving, because Ab was likely to fall asleep before he got ten miles out of Oklahoma City. Ab promised Margaret that they wouldn't go to a rodeo if they couldn't afford a motel.

"He kept his word all but one time," Margaret recalled. "We stopped in a town where there weren't any motels. We slept in the horse trailer until it started raining. The trailer wasn't enclosed so we headed for the pickup. Ab grabbed his saddle and blankets out of the back of the truck and put them in the cab with us. I looked a mess and smelled like wet horse blankets the next morning when we got to the rodeo grounds. Thank goodness one of the cowboy's wives invited me to their place to clean up."

Ab and Margaret wanted children, but Margaret had two miscarriages. They decided to adopt and it was a joyous day when Abbott Joseph joined the Deakins family.

When Little Ab, as he was called, reached school age he carried on the Deakins tradition by enrolling at Crooked Oak. His grandfather had served on the school board, when the school was just a wooden building.

Little Ab loved rodeo life as much as his parents did and began roping when he was in grade school. Many times Ab Sr. couldn't take him to miniature shows, so Margaret took him.

"It about killed me the first time we went and he didn't win anything. He was so disappointed and shed a few tears. I told him to keep practicing and he would be a winner some day. It wasn't long before he was winning and having a great time."

Little Ab roped in the high school rodeo finals and was on the rodeo team at Oklahoma State University. He continued roping after college and one of his sons also carried on the tradition.

Margaret and Ab traveled mostly close to home, as Ab had a business to run. Margaret loved going to Cheyenne, Wyoming to the Frontier Days Celebration. The Calcutta at the Lazy E arena in Guthrie, Oklahoma was another favorite rodeo. Margaret and some of her friends would pool their money and buy a roper. If he did well in the roping, they won a bit of money.

"I loved the National Finals Rodeo in Oklahoma City, and was one of a group of ladies to organize a style show in which wives of the cowboys modeled," Margaret said. "We were all members of the Rodeo Historical Society and quite active in all aspects of rodeo. The group first met in a private home, but the next year we met and held the style show at a Holiday Inn. We always had a drawing during the style show and some very nice prizes were given. One year I won a Fredrick Remington oil painting. Another year I won a leather saddle purse."

Andy and Jean Curtis were well-known rodeo personalities and instrumental in many activities held while the National Finals was in Oklahoma City. They hosted a party at their home for *Ketchpen* members.

"They had wonderful parties in their lovely home. The guys really loved it because the bar stool seats were saddles."

The Gold Card Room was available at each National Finals performance. This room was for PRCA members and their families. All kinds of food and drinks were provided, and while friends visited, they could watch the rodeo on a big screen television.

Margaret kept a guest book one year for those visiting the Gold Card Room. "I had lots of names the first night and was looking forward to keeping the book again the second night. When I asked for it, one of the helpers told me it had been stolen. I was just sick. They never kept a book again."

Ab retired from professional rodeo in 1970, but not from rodeo. He joined the Old Timers Rodeo Association and did quite well. He won saddles, trophies, and buckles, and served as president for several years.

Margaret was elected queen of the organization in 1971. "We had a ball those last years that Ab roped. And my, what good friends we have made over the years."

The Deakins' home was a popular place. The bunkhouse served as home away from home for many cowboys. During the week of the Finals, Margaret and Ab had a house full and loved every minute of it.

"Little Ab stayed in the bunkhouse when he was older and doing a lot of rodeoing by himself. I never knew who might show up at the breakfast table or how many horses would be in the pasture."

Friends still drop by, but Margaret's life is much different now that Ab is gone. They were married over fifty years and spent very little time apart.

"We had a good life and so much fun. My fondest memories are of days spent with our rodeo family. Ab wasn't the best, but he was good enough to compete and no one loved to rope anymore than he did."

Ab Jr. and his wife Sheri lived in Oklahoma City. Their three children, Joseph Abbott (Jad), Brant Ward, and Shanna Tae are grown and married. Jad and his wife have one son, Kaden Abbott. They check on Margaret often and she is very proud of them.

Margaret continued to lend a helping hand when able. A young man attending her church once needed a place to stay while he was in school. Margaret let him stay in the bunkhouse. They attended church together and he helped her around the place. He stayed two years and then entered the seminary in St. Louis, Missouri. He went on to pastor a church in New York and stayed in touch with Margaret.

When Ab's sister died, Margaret inherited his parents' property. She allowed a college student, who took care of the yard, to move into the house. Upon graduation, he became an X-ray technician at McBride Bone and Joint Hospital in Oklahoma City. He lived in the house until 2003. "He mows or trims trees, whatever I need done," Margaret said.

Bad health slowed Margaret a bit, but as of 2006 she still drove herself to church and to the doctor.

"I don't go and do a lot anymore," she admitted, "but I try to stay busy and keep my mind occupied. If I get bored or lonely I pick up a book and read. Nothing like a good book to take your mind off things."

Ask Margaret a question about rodeo, and a twinkle would appear in her eye to go with an ever-present smile.

Margaret Deakins riding a paint horse on the family
farm near Shawnee, Oklahoma.

Margaret Deakins standing with Ab Deakins' roping horse, Barney.

Ab and Margaret Deakins in rodeo grounds parking lot following a Senior Rodeo.

National Finals Rodeo Ladies Day in Oklahoma City
(1972). Left to right: Nell Shaw, (unknown), Margaret
Deakins, Jean Curtis, (unknown).

III

Jo
Ramsey Decker

"MY dad loved to buy and sell ranches," Jo said.

"When my twin brother, Jack, and I were just about school age Dad bought a ranch in Old Mexico. We left our ranch in San Angelo, Texas and drove to Torreon, Mexico. From Torreon we caught an ore train to the Promontory Mines, then rode horseback twenty-five miles to the ranch. I carried a case of *Coca-Cola* in front of my saddle. I was a coke-alcoholic and didn't think that I could survive without them."

Riding was no problem for the Ramsey twins. They began riding goats in the yard when they were young, and then graduated to horses. Their governess and teacher, Marguerite, accompanied them.

The ranch was large and joined Pancho Villa's land on one side. Jo and Jack rode and worked along side their dad when they weren't in class with Marguerite. Mrs. Ramsey, Ruby, didn't care much for riding. She enjoyed cooking and keeping house for her family. Jo's uncles were frequent visitors. She later decided they were coming to visit the beautiful Marguerite more than their own family.

The Ramsey family lived on the ranch for about four years then moved back to San Angelo, Texas. Over the years they would live on ranches in Texas, Oklahoma, Arkansas, New Mexico, and Old Mexico. Jo was in her teens when her dad bought a dude ranch in Arkansas.

"I was old enough to be a lot of help on the ranch. One of my favorite jobs was taking horses to the river and exercising them. I rode one horse and led four others. After tying up the extra horses, I'd ride one and swim him in the river until he got tired. Then switch and get a fresh horse. I'd hold onto their mane or tail and let them pull me along as they swam. It was great fun for me and good exercise for the horses."

Mr. Ramsey was also into producing rodeos at this time. He hired a man named Paul Bond to help keep books for him at a rodeo in Memphis, Tennessee. Jo was about thirteen at this time and interested in everything involved in rodeo. Paul began teaching her the responsibilities of a rodeo secretary. Later that year she was hired as secretary for a local rodeo.

"I doubt he would have hired me if he had known my age," Jo admitted. "Thanks to Paul's training I did just fine."

Jo loved every aspect of rodeo. She rode in her first rodeo in Alpine, Texas when she was only four years old. By the 1940s she had won cowgirl contests, awards, and saddles in three states. In 1944 she graduated from high school in Sallisaw, Oklahoma. That same year she was chosen as ranch girl of the year. This award enabled her to attend the rodeo at Madison Square Garden in New York City. She won the award again in 1946 making her only one of two girls to win the honor twice.

"Being chosen ranch girl of the year was one of the biggest thrills of my life."

Well known as an accomplished horsewoman, Jo was often asked to show horses for people. In March of 1946, she was showing a horse in Fort Worth, Texas. Once, after leaving the show ring to put away her horse, she then sat on the fence in the alleyway to wait for the next event.

"Jack Wade walked up to me and introduced Tater Decker, a

cowboy from Roswell, New Mexico," Jo recalled. "We talked for a while and Tater asked me for a date. I wasn't familiar with dating, but accepted his invitation. He later told me that he decided to marry me the minute he spotted me sitting on the fence in that beautiful red western outfit topped off with a white hat. When we went out the second time, Tater asked me to marry him. I made him wait until November."

Jo and Tater continued to date and rodeo. They married November 20, 1946.

Before they married, H. D. Binns was contracting the stock for the rodeo at Dewey, Oklahoma, which is held on July 4th every year. He hired Jo for her first official rodeo secretary job. She would serve as rodeo secretary for twenty-five years. Some of the contractors she worked for were Albert Harris, Gene Autry and Everett Colborn's Lighting C Rodeo Company, Harry Knight, Hoss Inman, Harry Vold, and Mike Cervi. When Lynn Beutler approached her with a two-year contract, she agreed but only for two years. She ended up working for the stock contractor for twenty years.

"We became good friends and I never worked for anyone nicer than Lynn Beutler."

Many times Jo drove for Lynn and his wife. They would drive all night to make it on time for the next rodeo. When they arrived, Lynn would get Jo a room and she would sleep until time to go to work. Her job was to collect entry fees, type the names of all the contestants and what events they entered. All of the livestock were numbered, and those numbers were drawn and given to a cowboy. For example, each bucking horse was numbered and that number was recorded and placed in a hat. When the entry time was closed and the list of bronc riders recorded, a number was drawn and given to each cowboy. This was done for every event, except the women's barrel racing.

Since contestants didn't compete in every performance, they called Jo to find out when they were scheduled. Most of the time they would call collect and ask for themselves. Jo would say, "We expect him such and such night." The cowboy then knew when he was to be there to perform.

During the rodeo, Jo often acted as flag bearer. Then she dismounted and climbed into the announcer's booth to keep and record times, answer questions, and sometimes settle disputes. At the end of each performance, she figured the day money and the average. She calculated all of the winnings and wrote the checks.

Tater and Jo could usually travel together, but there were times when he would finish at a rodeo and she had to remain until it was over. He traveled on to another rodeo. Many times Jo was out late, especially if she had to work the slack after the main rodeo was over. It was a little scary to walk to the hotel or to her car in the wee hours of the morning. When word got out that Tater wasn't with her some of the cowboys hung around and just happened to be there when she finished with her work.

"They escorted me to my hotel and made sure that I was safe," Jo recalled. "If there was a dance after the rodeo, they would beg me to go, so they would have someone to dance with. I wasn't too hard to persuade because I loved to dance. All the young cowboys called me Mama Jo and treated me like I was family."

When Jo and Tater traveled together they stayed with friends, family, or in a motel. They were much too busy to worry about settling in one spot. One time when they were at a rodeo in Lubbock, Texas, Tater was entered in five events: saddle bronc, bareback bronc, calf roping, steer wrestling, and bull riding. He placed in every event. Sometime during the rodeo he learned that there was a rodeo starting on Friday in Roseburg, Oregon and they were giving $500 to the all around winner. When he told Jo about the rodeo, she said, "Let's go." They loaded up the horse, and away they went. Tater won both rounds in the saddle bronc event and the calf roping. He split third and fourth in the bareback riding, and won second in the steer wrestling. When he went to collect his winnings, they counted out $500 in five-dollar bills. He carried the money to the car in a paper sack, put it in the trunk and hit the road to the next rodeo.

In 1950 Jo's uncle died, leaving a young widow and three small children. Worried about how her aunt was going to support herself and her children, Jo came up with a plan to design and sell western wear.

"I made my own stuff, and everyone commented they wanted me to make their clothes. I didn't have time to do that. I thought that maybe I could design outfits and let Aunt Estelle sell them from her home."

Jo went to drafting school and learned to draw patterns then started designing western clothing. *Jo Decker Originals* became an instant hit. Soon Jo moved Estelle and the business to a shop in San Angelo. Sta's Western Togs offered custom made suits, shirts, and pants, Don Hoy hats, chaps, belts, and boots, leather and silver pony tail clips.

Jo's designs became so popular that singing and entertainment stars began having her design outfits for them. Rex Allen, Rose Maddox, Lynn Anderson, and even the late Princess Grace of Monaco special ordered *Jo Decker Originals*. Neiman Marcus had a special Jo Decker section in their store and often held showings for her in Dallas and Houston.

In 1953 Tater and Jo still hadn't found a permanent place to hang their hats. They stayed with friends and family as they traveled around the country. Jo's folks bought a ranch near Clayton, Oklahoma. When the ranch adjoining their property came up for sale, Tater and Jo thought that it would be the perfect place for them. They bought the ranch and built a house.

"We had our dining room suit handmade in Old Mexico," Jo said. "The table was twelve feet long and the chairs had tall backs and were beautifully carved. I spruced up the kitchen with a red refrigerator and stove. Finally we had a place to hang our pictures and set our trophies. One chest of drawers housed loose rodeo pictures that we didn't have room to hang. The house burned and we lost almost everything. We rebuilt but will never be able to replace all the wonderful pictures that we lost."

Because of Jo's reputation as a hard worker and an excellent secretary, she was asked to serve as production coordinator for the first National Finals Rodeo held in Dallas, Texas in the fall of 1959. Her job was to plan the opening ceremonies for ten performances and to carry the American flag for each.

"I went to Dallas a month before the start of the NFR. There was no one to designate the work to, so I did it myself. It was very hard work, but I wouldn't trade it for anything. Looking back, it was a wonderful experience."

She served as secretary or timer for the National Finals Rodeo seven times in the late 1960s and early 1970s.

The rodeo held at Madison Square Garden in New York City was another big event for which Jo planned the publicity and opening ceremonies. Again, she would go weeks early and work to put everything together and act as spokesperson to promote the rodeo.

"I usually went to New York City a couple of weeks before the rodeo started. There was lots of advertising on the radio and meetings at various places. Believe me I stayed busy every minute, but truly loved my job."

Tater continued to ride broncs, rope calves, and steer wrestle. He didn't ride bulls often because they made his muscles sore, and that affected his other events. He competed for about twenty-five years. In those years he won the bronc riding at Madison Square Garden; the bulldogging at Cheyenne, Wyoming; the bareback riding at Houston, Texas; and the all around title three times at Colorado Springs, Colorado. He qualified for the National Finals several times and was inducted into the Cowboy Hall of fame in Oklahoma City, Oklahoma, in 1992. He was also an inductee in the Pikes Peak or Bust Hall of Fame in Colorado Springs, Colorado, and the National Senior Pro Rodeo Association Hall of Fame.

The Deckers' were involved in rodeo for about twenty years before they added a passenger. Their son, Dirk Ramsey, joined the team in 1969 and immediately began traveling with his parents.

"He rode many miles on a pillow in the floorboard of the car. When we arrived at a rodeo and I went to work, one of the cowboy's wives kept him for me. One rodeo I couldn't find a single woman that I knew and Tater was busy getting ready for his events. Hearing of my plight, here came those big old wonderful cowboys to take care of Dirk. They just passed him around from one to another and did a fine job."

Tater retired from competition but worked for Beutler Brothers as a pickup man until Jo retired. Retirement meant changing jobs. They began selling racehorse tack at tracks in Denver, Colorado and Albuquerque, Raton and Ruidoso, New Mexico. Dirk attended school wherever they happened to be and did fine.

Eventually, Tater and Jo trained a horse and began running him. His name was Two Step Louis. His sire was the famous Kentucky Derby winner Valiant Dancer. One year they ran him in seven races. He won five firsts and two seconds. During his career he won twelve firsts.

Between racing seasons, the family returned to their ranch.

They ran about 150 head of cattle on approximately 1,000 acres. Dirk helped on the ranch and began to show interest in rodeo competition. When he was ten, he entered the Little Britches rodeo events and was an all around champion. He was also high school rodeo champion and went to college in Durant, Oklahoma, on a rodeo and academic scholarship. Dirk, his wife Misty, and their daughter Harley J. moved within *hollering* distance of his parents, where Dirk raised Mexican cattle used for team roping and opened a business in Talihina, Oklahoma.

After really retiring, Jo became a member of the local county fair board. She served on the board for nine years. Using her organizational and promotional skills, the board went from broke to raising enough funds to construct a new county fair barn. The structure was dedicated as the Jo Decker County Fair Building.

Jo received many awards over the years. Among them was the "Tad Lucas Award" presented each year at the National Cowboy and Western Heritage Hall of Fame in Oklahoma City to an outstanding woman in rodeo.

Tad Lucas had been an All-Around Champion Cowgirl for eight years. When women's events were discontinued, she trick rode for another twenty-five years as a contract performer. Following her death in 1990, her family established the Tad Lucas award with an endowment from her estate. Jo received the award in 1999. She was inducted into the Cowboy Hall of Fame in 2000 for her work as rodeo secretary. She is also an inductee in the Pikes Peak or Bust Hall of Fame, the Pro Rodeo Hall of Fame in Colorado Springs, and The Texas Rodeo Hall of Fame in Belton, Texas.

Jo served on the Rodeo Historical Society Board from 1996-1999. She is a Gold Card Holder of the PRCA, a member of the American Quarter Horse Association, Rodeo Cowboy Alumni Association, and the Rodeo Historical Society.

The Deckers remained active in rodeo activities. They seldom missed the National Finals, and tried to attend all of the Rodeo Cowboy Alumni Association meetings. The Rodeo Cowboy Alumni Association was formed in 1988 to support and promote the sport of rodeo as well as to keep former contestants, fans, and friends in touch with each other. Every year this organization gave scholarships to two high school seniors who had participated in high school rodeo and made it to the finals. These scholarships were given in memory of Lane Frost and John R. Hatley.

Over the many years in the rodeo business, Jo and Tater have formed lasting friendships. Sometimes the highway seemed non-ending and the work overpowering, but once everyone met to begin another rodeo, it was worth the effort.

Jo and Tater's home was once again filled with rodeo trophies, buckles, and pictures of the talented two, friends, and of their son, and his family.

It has been said that Jo's success as a rodeo secretary came from her ability to understand problems, whether it was with cowboys or judges or stock contractors, and then come up with solutions. Willingness to work hard and go that extra mile, both in the arena and out, contributed to her many achievements.

Jo Decker taking a break (circa 1945).

Jo Decker working as a rodeo secretary, talking to
Torrie Conley Curtis.

Jo Decker as flag bearer (and production coordinator)
at the National Finals Rodeo in Dallas, Texas (1959).

Jo and Tater Decker modeling Jo's western wear designs.

Tater, Jo, and son Dirk Decker in Oklahoma City, when Jo was presented the Tad Lucas Award.

Ladies modeling Jo's western designs at the 1964
National Finals Rodeo in Los Angeles.

Left to right: Torrie Conley Curtis, Jo Ann Jones,
Jo Decker (Center), June Ivory, and Corky Randall.

IV

Decie
Nowlin Goodspeed

"YOU bet we had running water," Decie said.

"Mama handed us a bucket and said run. That meant a quick trip to the spring and back. Seemed like one of us kids was running for water constantly. We also carried water to the seedbeds so that we would have something to plant when gardening time came. The spring furnished water for all of our needs plus provided a place to keep our butter cool. The butter crock was taken to the spring every morning and placed in the shallow water. Every evening it was carried back to the house for safe keeping at night."

The Nowlin family consisted of George and his wife Eliza, and their six children: Ilah, Odie, Harvey, Decie, Ella, and Orville. Two other children, Jasper and Audra died in infancy. Home was a double log house that sat at the bottom of Crow Mountain in Pope County Arkansas.

"I didn't realize that we were poor. We always had enough to eat and a change or two of clothes. Every fall we each got a new pair of shoes to wear to school. I felt very fortunate because many kids didn't have shoes and couldn't walk to school in the winter."

George Nowlin farmed cotton, corn, sorghum cane and enough tobacco for personal use. Eliza raised a vegetable garden and a large orchard furnished a variety of fruit.

"I don't ever remember having money. Dad would charge the things we needed at Clifton's store then pay his bill when he sold his crops. Shoes, flour, and baking powder were some of the things that he charged. Once in a while, he would buy us an orange or banana and some nuts for Christmas. Candy was a rare treat. I guess that's the reason I didn't have a cavity until I was fifty-five years old."

There was a one-room church that most of the people on Crow Mountain attended. Decie remembers going to church with her family and then many of the neighbors would gather at the Nowlins' house for the afternoon. The men sat on the porch and discussed religion or crops while the women fixed lunch. There were many children and they loved to play in the barn or down by the creek. Decie's Uncle Billy and Aunt Lucy had seventeen kids.

"We were always busy hoeing, planting, gathering, canning-- whatever was necessary to survive," Decie said. "One of my jobs was to help Harvey put the peaches out to dry. Mama would give us a clean white sheet to lay on top of the seed house. We would pick the peaches, take out the seeds, and lay the peach halves on the sheet to dry in the sun. Every evening we had to gather the peaches and put them inside. After the dew was gone the next morning, we put them on the roof again. I don't know why that was always my job."

In addition to farming, Mr. Nowlin cut timber and hauled it to the sawmill to be cut into boards. He built the house, and then added on an extra room as the family increased in number. Some years there wasn't enough money from his crops to pay his debt so he cut timber and sold it to make up the difference.

Eliza was known as the medicine woman in the community. She was called upon to tend the sick and prepare the dead for burial. When word was sent that she was needed she gathered up the necessary items and called for Decie.

"I guess she chose me because I was bossy and could manage the kids."

While Eliza cared for the body, someone else would sew the shroud and the men would build a coffin. Decie's job was to keep the children out of the way. She usually did that by putting them to work.

"I'd make sure all the water buckets were full and there was plenty of wood for the stove. Little kids can do those kinds of things. The older girls and I would scrub the kitchen and sometimes prepare a meal. I kept them hopping."

"On one occasion Mama was washing the body and a woman was sewing the shroud on a very noisy sewing machine. The machine clattered on and on grinding on nerves. Finally, she paused to adjust the material. An old gentleman said, "My God. Pearl's making enough noise to wake the dead." Despite the solemn occasion everyone had a good laugh at the unintentional humor."

The family had its share of accidents and illness, but all survived. Odie was bitten on the foot by a copperhead snake. Eliza soaked his foot in coal oil until green foam formed on top of the liquid. Then she cleaned his foot and sent him on his way. He didn't even get sick. When Decie was eight Odie accidentally hit her in the right eye with a piece of wire. Mr. Nowlin took her to the doctor but there was nothing he could do to save her sight.

"I almost lost my mind that summer. It was hard to adjust to being blind in that eye. Odie hated so much that it had happened but I never held it against him."

In 1928 sixteen-year-old Decie helped load her uncle's truck. Cottonseed filled the bottom of the truck bed and the canned goods were placed in it to keep them from breaking. Decie and Ella squeezed in as best they could and the drive to Oklahoma began. Mr. Nowlin and Odie hauled the furniture in a wagon pulled by a team of horses.

One of Decie's friends remarked "I'd like to be moving west, maybe I could marry a cowboy."

"I thought that was the stupidest thing I'd ever heard."

The family moved to the community of Qusada in Okfuskee County and rented a farm. Decie attended Qusada School for a short time then went to live with her sister Ilah in Seminole. Some of Decie's fondest memories are of the days she spent with her sister and her family.

During her years in Seminole, she babysat with her niece and nephew, worked for a family named Harberson and attended Seminole High School. This was quite an adjustment for a girl from Arkansas, but she worked hard and graduated in 1932.

Decie was surprised when her dad gave her the money to buy a senior ring. This was during the *Great Depression*, and she knew they didn't have much money. She later learned that her dad and her younger sister, Ella, had picked up pecans and sold them so that Decie could have a ring. What they didn't know was that Decie had used her own hard-earned money to buy her married brother a pair of shoes.

While she was going to school, Decie dated some city boys and a couple of the guys were pretty serious about her. She never dreamed that a ranch hand would enter her life. She was visiting her parents one weekend when her mother sent her to a neighbor's house for a corn relish recipe. That neighbor happened to be Mrs. Dobbs, Buck Goodspeed's mother.

The first problem was that Decie didn't like to ride, but Mrs. Dobbs lived about four miles away. Wearing a pair of blue-striped pants that she had made and of which she was quite proud, Decie took off on old Dan to get the recipe. She made the ride over without incident got the recipe and Mrs. Dobbs gave her a pound of butter. Buck was leaning against a tree whittling when she left the house and started for her horse.

"I'll trade britches with you," he said.

"I thought that was a forward thing to say, and it just made me furious," says Decie, "so I gave him a go-to-hell look and started to mount up. When I put my weight on the stirrup it fell off and I almost took a tumble. I tried to fix it but wasn't having much luck."

Buck ambled over and said, "Why don't you let me do that?"

He worked on the stirrup then said, "I don't think this is going to hold, so I'll give you a hand up."

Decie wasn't sure what "hand up" meant.

Realizing her confusion Buck laughed and put his hands together, so she could put her foot in them. The make shift stirrup worked and Decie was happy to be mounted and able to get away. About a mile down the road, a dog scared Dan and the other stirrup came loose. She managed to catch it and finished the trip home carrying the stirrup and butter.

Buck continued to date other girls and Decie was still working in Seminole during the week, but she often came home on weekends. Seems like Buck happened around most of the weekends she was home. She later found out that Jess, Buck's younger brother, was keeping Buck informed about what Decie was doing. Jess was dating Decie's sister, Ella.

Decie wasn't sure about Buck. He was used to women falling all over themselves for him. She wasn't impressed that he was a cowboy, and she didn't like the fact that he wore jeans all of the time. The men she had been dating wore dress clothes.

He finally talked her into going to a goat roping with him. "I didn't have a very good time. It was hot, dusty, and I didn't understand what was going on. I did find out that Buck was a very good roper. I thought that he was just showing off and didn't offer any comment on the subject."

Decie enjoyed visiting Buck's family. They were friendly and seemed to love company. She remembers that they had candy and nuts, things that she didn't have at home. Buck's little sister, told Decie that Buck was showing off for her.

Decie returned the favor and invited Buck to her house for dinner. She baked biscuits for the occasion. Buck made quite a hand with the biscuits. Decie's little brother observed him for a while and then commented, "Boy, you sure like them biscuits, don't you?" Decie was ready to kill him. Later that evening Buck asked her out on a real date.

As Decie and Buck began to spend more time together, her opinion of him began to change. He was dependable and showed a great deal of respect for her, plus he was quite handsome. Decie's Aunt Suze got her attention when she said, "Oh, that's the purtiest man I've ever seen in my life. I'd marry him if I was you."

Decie liked to dance but Buck didn't. However, he agreed to take her to a local dance one Saturday night. All was going well and Decie was dancing with different guys while Buck watched. One boy kept asking her to dance after she told him several times that she was going to sit out for awhile. When he came back and asked again, he suddenly found himself flat on his back on the floor. Buck looked down at him, saying, "She said she didn't want to dance." They didn't attend any more dances after that.

Decie didn't understand the concept of rodeo and, even though Buck was winning a considerable amount of prize money, she wanted him to have a steady job. He told her that if she would marry him he would go to Fort Worth and win enough money to get them started. Then he would quit rodeoing and go to work on a ranch. That way they would have a steady income and a place to live.

The night of the rodeo Decie went to her neighbors to listen to the Fort Worth competition on the radio. The neighbor's weren't as interested and kept switching the station to Ma Perkins, so she didn't know until he came home that he hadn't placed. He did collect mount money from cowboys riding his horse and they were married on March 14th in 1934.

They were leaving the courthouse after the ceremony when they heard someone hollering from the third story. It was Jerry Littrell, one of Buck's buddies. He had spent the night in jail. Jerry called out, "Hey Buck! Did somebody finally get you?"

When they stopped in Henryetta, Decie stayed in the car while Buck went into Whippett's Men's Store to buy some pajamas. People kept coming by looking at the car and then laughing. She thought they were laughing at her but when she asked Buck he held up a 'Just Married' sign that had been attached to the car.

Buck spent the rest of the day helping his brother plant potatoes but his sister-in-law prepared a nice dinner and baked a wedding cake for the newlyweds. The next morning Buck went to work with his brother Carl while Decie set up housekeeping.

Decie had some things that she had received at a shower but not everything they needed. Buck gave her $100 to spend. With that $100 she bought a living room suite, a rocking chair, a library table, a kitchen cabinet, some sheets and pillowcases, and some dishes.

There was plenty of food but no money. One day Decie asked Buck for money to buy a stamp. He didn't have any money at all. That prompted him to begin practicing roping at a friend's place in Okmulgee.

He practiced on Sunday, which was his day off, but his brother didn't approve and told him to quit. When he went to work Monday morning after ignoring his brother's orders, he was told he would have to quit roping on Sundays if he wanted to keep his job.

Buck and his younger brother Jess quit working on the Moore Ranch on the spot. He brought the car and trailer back to the house and told Decie, "Pack up. We're out of here." Decie was so upset that she started crying. Buck tried to comfort her by telling her he could make more at one rodeo than he could in a month on the ranch. She wasn't convinced.

The couple moved in with Buck's family. Although Buck's mother, Mrs. Dobbs, was good to her, Decie wanted a home of her own. She certainly wanted her own home when she learned that she was pregnant. Sick and dissatisfied she went to Seminole and stayed with her sister. When Buck came after her, she refused to go with him. "I'll come back when I have a house to come home to," she had told him.

When he came back the next time, it was with news that they had a house and that it was all cleaned up and ready for her. She told him where to put the furniture. Sure enough, when she stepped through the front door everything was just as she had requested.

Decie wasn't far along in her pregnancy when she became very ill. She lost down to eighty pounds and passed out at times. It became necessary for her to move back in with Mr. and Mrs. Dobbs, so they could help care for her. She finally got to see her doctor when he returned from a trip to Arkansas. Decie made it through nine miserable months, and Janice Annette was born August 4, 1935.

Janice was the first baby in the group of rodeo couples that Buck and Decie ran around with so Buck was nicknamed "Pappy." He was called by that name throughout his rodeo career.

Buck was making a good living and Decie began to enjoy attending rodeos with him. She enjoyed having her hair done and dressing up for these events. Buck would escort her and find a good seat for her before he left to compete.

"He treated me like a lady and I appreciated that."

Pregnant with their second child, Decie went into labor on September 29, 1937. Sonny was born early enough that morning for Buck to go to the Muskogee State Fair rodeo. He later told someone that was the greatest day of his life, a baby boy, new horse and winning a roping all in the same day.

Their youngest child, Judy was born April 24, 1943. Although the pregnancy had been better than the previous two, Decie's physician didn't want her to have any more children. Judy was delivered by Cesarean section.

Buck and Decie worked out a pretty good routine in which they shared chores. She went with him to the arena and let the calves or steers out for him. He helped with the dishes and housecleaning.

"Rodeo competition is like any other sport," Decie said. "You have to practice every day. You can't just show up and compete."

They would practice until lunch and then go to town or to visit neighbors until it was time for the kids to get home from school. Buck usually practiced again in the evening.

Sunday afternoons when Buck was home, folks gathered at the Goodspeed arena to practice and have fun. There would be calf roping, steer roping, steer wrestling, and steer riding. The little kids could participate in calf riding if they were brave enough.

A basketball court complete with two goals and boundaries marked with flour from Decie's kitchen saw lots of action. Young and old alike played. Another favorite game was Annie Over.

In the winter neighbors would bring a dish of some kind and after a good meal play dominoes or cards.

Traveling was a new experience to Decie and her younger sister Ella. Ella married Jess, Buck's younger brother, and the couples attended many rodeos together. As well as making shows in Oklahoma, they went to places like Ft. Worth, Texas; Phoenix, Arizona; Cheyenne and Sheridan, Wyoming; Greeley, Colorado; and Chicago, Illinois.

Decie enjoyed the rodeo at Dewey, Oklahoma. Every Fourth-of-July, Buck, Decie, and the kids traveled to Dewey and rented a cabin on Caney Creek. They became good friends with the cabin owners and looked forward to seeing them each year. The cabins were nice and there were places for the kids to play. One year the owner gave Buck and Decie's son Sonny and Jess and Ella's son Bobby a bunch of fireworks. The boys went to the tavern across the creek and threw some firecrackers inside the building. When fireworks started popping, tavern patrons came pouring out the door. Needless to say, the boys thought it was much funnier than the tavern patrons did.

Summer meant Decie and the kids could travel with Buck. The rules were discussed before arriving at their destination. There would be no running around. Any playing would be done in the area where they were seated. You had a choice of a bottle of pop or a candy bar, but not both. There was no fighting, bickering, or horsing around in the car. Each child had their area and they were to stay in it.

Many rodeo families camped out when attending rodeos. However, Buck told Decie that they would rent rooms when they traveled. "If we can't afford to do that, we just won't go," he said. To cut down on expenses they tried to rent rooms with cooking facilities.

The Fort Worth Rodeo lasted for two weeks and there was a calf roping every night. It was one of Buck and Decie's favorites because while there they stayed with their good friends, the Holidays. Buck won first place there twice.

Decie shopped for Easter outfits at Lerner's in Fort Worth. She would take the children one at a time, while Buck kept an eye on the others. When the children were outfitted, Decie shopped for herself. Buck even got in on the shopping one year and left Decie with the kids while he shopped for himself.

The first year they went to Chicago, they stayed at Mrs. McDermott's rooming house on Washington Boulevard, and stayed there each year afterward.

Sonny and Janice were small, so Buck hired a neighbor girl to go with them to Chicago to stay with the kids. That allowed Decie to go to the rodeo with Buck and to do some sightseeing. Mrs. McDermott's daughter, Helen, took Decie and Ella downtown at midnight. They were impressed with the lights and the landmark buildings. Another time, Helen took them to the bargain basement in a large department store. Two women grabbed the same garment and got into a struggle over it. They pulled at the garment so hard that they tore it. When the clerk expected payment for the torn item, no one would admit they had even touched it. Decie and Ella were shocked. Decie said, "It looked like a scene out of a movie."

Decie and Ella became comfortable shopping and doing their own thing when in Chicago. Their Oklahoma accent drew lots of attention and teasing. Friends cautioned them to be watchful in a big city for people who would take advantage of them. One day Decie and Ella were talking and laughing as they walked down the street. They were window shopping and going from place to place.

Decie noticed a man following them. They hatched up a plan. Decie said, "We'll stop at the door of that store just ahead, but not go in. He'll have to go on past. If he grabs you, I'll take off my shoe and work him over. You do the same if he grabs me." They stopped as planned, but the man went on by.

Mrs. McDermott laughed when they told her about the incident. She said, "I don't think he meant you any harm. He was probably just getting a kick out of listening to the way you two talk."

One of the guys in the rooming house made a pass at Decie. She told him to keep his mouth shut or her husband would beat hell out of him. When she went out to hang her laundry, someone pecked on a window. Of course, she looked to see what was happening. It was the guy's wife standing there naked. "Man was I shocked," Decie said. "Later, someone pecked on the window again but I didn't look this time. I was afraid it might be the guy standing there this time."

After the kids were old enough to go to school, Decie didn't get to travel with Buck. She and the kids did the farm chores and took care of the cattle. Decie was extremely afraid of storms. If the weather was questionable, she gathered the kids and went to the cellar. Many evenings the four spent the night in the cellar. It was comfortable there because Buck had built a bed large enough for all of them, and there were lamps for light. She remembers one time when a storm came up just as supper was ready. "We filled our plates and ate supper in the cellar."

Two different times Decie had premonitions that something was wrong. The first time she dreamed that someone was wounded, and she was trying to get to the person who was hurt. Someone was holding a heavy piece of red and black striped cloth. When Buck came home, he brought her a black and red striped rug. That didn't explain the wounded person. Buck later told her about getting into a fight with a guy who cheated him on his time. The man hit Buck behind the ear with a closed pocketknife causing a cut and a knot on his head.

Buck's most serious injury happened July 8, 1951. He was in a match roping with Ike Rude at Waynoka, Oklahoma. It was a windy day and Decie would find out later that when Buck roped his steer the wind caught the slack in the rope and blew it under his horse. The horse's front legs became entangled in the rope. When the steer on the other end of the rope took out the slack, it jerked the horse's feet out from under him. The horse fell and rolled completely over. The saddle horn hit Buck in the head.

Decie had sensed something was wrong before she left for the roping. She and Judy rode up with Dr. Cochran, a friend of the family. They arrived after the roping had started and immediately looked for Buck. Ace Soward, a family friend, was flagging and saw Decie at the fence. He handed the flag to another cowboy and told her what had happened. He then went with them to the hospital.

Buck was unconscious. Dr. Cochran didn't agree with the treatment they were giving him and told Decie they needed to get him out of there. Arrangements were made to transfer him to St. Anthony's Hospital in Oklahoma City. On the way the ambulance broke down and the driver had to call for another ambulance. During the wait, Buck began vomiting and Dr. Cochran told Decie to pray because he was afraid that Buck might not live. They finally arrived in Oklahoma City at 4:00 a.m. the next morning.

When he was settled in his room, Decie prayed: "If it be thy will, let this cup pass." Instantly, a cup came through the door, passed over Buck's bed, and then disappeared through the wall. Real or imagined, surely it was a sign that he would live. He did open his eyes the next day but didn't speak. Everyone tried to get Decie to leave, but she stayed steadfast by Buck's side.

Decie stayed with him night and day for thirteen days, sleeping in a chair beside his bed. Her stay in Oklahoma City wasn't pleasant. The doctors and nurses were unkind and she was upset. One day she caught a glance of herself in the mirror and realized that she looked a mess.

"No wonder the doctor won't listen to you," she said to herself.

Using three bobby pins, she curled her hair as best she could, fixed her face, and squared her shoulders. Thirteen days later Buck was transferred to the hospital in Okemah.

Buck was still a very sick man when he came home from the hospital. He was to have absolute bed-rest, so Decie and the kids took over managing the farm. Janice was old enough to do the housework. Sonny and Decie took care of the cattle and crops. Judy was young, but helped when she could. It was over a year before Buck could work again.

During her husband's illness, Decie sold *Beauty Counselor* cosmetics. Mrs. Buryl Hopkins convinced her that she was a natural born sales person, and it proved to be true. She sold cosmetics until 1963, and then switched to *Sarah Coventry* jewelry. When Buck expressed regrets that she had to work, she explained how much she enjoyed the job and that people recognized the Goodspeed name because of him. Apparently, that made him feel better, because nothing more was said about it.

Eventually, Buck began to work for a construction company, and then gradually began to practice roping again. He did return to rodeo competition and often placed second or third. He worked hard but couldn't regain the strength and stamina he had before the accident. In 1956, Buck, Decie, and Judy drove to the Cheyenne rodeo. Decie was surprised when he asked her to drive. He had never let her drive pulling a trailer. He retired from rodeo after that summer.

When Decie first started traveling to rodeos with Buck, they had a 1932 Chevrolet convertible and a one horse trailer. "I guess you could call the trailer a convertible too, because it didn't have a top. We had to pull under a filling station awning one time to keep the horse from getting beat up in a hailstorm."

Later they drove a pickup with sideboards to haul the horse. After that a two door Chevy better accommodated their growing family. At night they found a motel and boarded the horse at the local stockyards.

Traveling wasn't easy. Decie quickly learned that Buck didn't stop until he needed gas. Nature calls were to be made then. After the kids started traveling with them, she carried crackers, a switch, water, and a pee pot.

"I learned to eat fast and not be demanding. We had lots of fun playing games and looking at the scenery. Looking back I am amazed that we traveled all those miles and never had an accident."

Buck loved to rodeo but he also loved to be home, and he loved to quail hunt. He didn't travel far away from Oklahoma. However, his roping horse Chigger often went to New York for the rodeo at Madison Square Garden. Buck could make as much money mounting cowboys, as he could going to the rodeo.

After years of marriage, Decie asked Buck if he had ever thought about leaving her when she had been so sick with each of her pregnancies.

"Yes, once," he had admitted.

"How long did you feel that way?" she asked.

"Couple of days," he answered.

They had a good life, if not always an easy one. Their home was a gathering place for kinfolk and other rodeo families. Many youngsters got an education in riding and roping in the Goodspeed arena, and enjoyed delicious meals at Decie's table.

"God has been good to me. He gave me knowledge to wait for the right man to share my life, and He gave me the strength to go through the bad times and not let them ruin the good. I have been blessed."

Decie and Buck Goodspeed celebrating their 50th wedding anniversary in 1984.

Decie Nowlin dressed for her High School graduation banquet in Seminole, Oklahoma (1932).

Buck and Decie Goodspeed with their children, Sonny and
Janice in Prescott, Arizona (1939).

Goodspeed family in Roswell, New Mexico (1947).
Clockwise from top left: Janice, Decie, Buck, Sonny,
and Judy (lower center).

Buck and Decie Goodspeed in their backyard near
Wetumka, Oklahoma (1971).

George Nowlin family in front of their log house in Pope County, Arkansas (1912). Left to right: Odie, Ilah, George, Harvey, and Eliza holding Decie as baby.

V

Jackie
Smith McEntire

JACQUELINE (Jackie) Smith grew up on a farm in the wooded hills of southeastern Oklahoma.

Hard work came naturally to the four Smith children: Imogene, Jackie, Dale, and Georgia. Their chores included caring for hogs, beef cattle, milk cows, horses and a variety of fowl. They raised feed crops for the animals and a vegetable garden provided food for the family.

"No one had much money, but we had plenty to eat," Jackie said. "Looking back I'd say we had a pretty good life. We worked hard but we had good times too. Most evenings after our chores were done, we got out the hymnbooks and sang. Music was always a big part of my life."

Jackie's mother, Reba Brasfield Smith, was from Smithville, Mississippi. When she was sixteen, her family moved to Wolf, Oklahoma. Included in the Brasfield family tree are Rod Brasfield, T. G. Shepherd, and C. B. (Fat) Irwin. C. B. worked for the

Pinkerton Agency and was also a professional cowboy. In 1933 he traveled the rodeo circuit with Clark McEntire's dad, John.

Elvin Smith, Jackie's father, grew up near Albion, Oklahoma. Elvin and Reba met at the Bethel Church and later married at Atoka. The couple lived in the Limestone Gap community in Atoka County.

Like most farm families, the Smith's social life centered on activities at the church and school. However, one of Jackie's favorite events was a fish fry held most summers. Several families would camp out near the creek and fish until they caught enough to feed everyone. Lard was melted in a big pot over the campfire. When it was piping hot, battered fish were dropped into the grease to fry. Large skillets of fried potatoes and bowls of fresh vegetables filled the makeshift tables set up under a shade tree. Sometimes someone would catch a soft-shelled turtle, cut it up and cook it with the fish.

"I still love to fish," Jackie said.

When Jackie was four, she began visiting school with her older sister Imogene. She loved to sing with the other children. Mrs. Stiewig, the primary grade teacher, was impressed with Jackie's singing and enjoyed putting on programs. She urged Mr. and Mrs. Smith to let her begin school. So at age four Jackie started to school and became an important part of school programs until she graduated from Limestone Gap High School at age sixteen.

Imogene and Jackie formed a quartet while they were in school. Along with Reda and Ruhama Springer, the girls sang at local churches and various other places.

Clark McEntire lived less than two miles from Jackie, but the families were part of different communities. The first Jackie heard of him was when Mrs. Stiewig borrowed some chaps and boots from Clark for Imogene to wear in a school program. Other than that, Jackie only remembered that he had attended Bethel Church a few times.

"I think he was mainly interested in checking out the girls. He didn't remember my singing. What caught his eye was my ability to carry two five-gallon buckets of slop to the hog pen."

Evidently Clark was impressed enough to pursue Jackie and they began dating. They courted for five years. During those years Jackie taught grades one through eight in a one-room schoolhouse.

Her salary was $65.00 per month, but improved later. Many of the students were bigger than she was, but she didn't have any discipline problems. She taught the way she lived: *work hard until your assignment is completed then we can all play together*. Jackie taught elementary grades for six years, and spent her final year teaching business at Limestone Gap High School. During her seven years of teaching, she walked or rode horseback to work.

Even though Clark had just gone broke in the cattle business, Jackie agreed to marry him. On March 17, 1950, the couple married in the Baptist parsonage at Atoka. As well as paying for the marriage license, Jackie bought a gold wedding band for three dollars down and three dollars a month.

Clark had borrowed a twenty-dollar bill from his mother, so he could pay the preacher. After the ceremony, Clark handed the twenty to the preacher expecting to get back some change. The preacher put the twenty in his pocket and thanked Clark kindly. There wasn't money for a honeymoon trip.

Both Jackie and Clark had cars when they married. Neither vehicle was paid for, so they decided to sell Jackie's green '49 Ford pickup and keep Clark's gas saving blue-gray '49 Studebaker car. Gas cost eighteen to twenty cents a gallon at that time.

"The reason it was a gas saver is because we spent more time pushing than driving, and I did most of the pushing!" Jackie recalled.

Their first house consisted of two rooms with a shed built on the back. It belonged to Clark's Uncle Keno and had been used as a hog house. They scrubbed it down with lye water, nailed deadening felt on the walls, and moved in.

They hadn't lived in the little house very long when Clark's mother died. Clark and Jackie moved in with Clark's father and lived with him for a little over a year. In September 1951 they moved into a three-room house near North Boggy Creek.

That summer would change many things for the McEntires. Clark and Jackie drove the undependable Studebaker to Carrollton, Texas, where Clark was entered in the calf roping competition. This was a big Fourth of July celebration and a new Ford car plus $700 cash would be awarded to the winner. Clark won the roping. Jackie was asked to drive the new car into the arena. She was so excited that she bumped the gate as she drove through.

"I felt like an idiot," she said.

Clark was loading up to head to Pendleton, Oregon, to a rodeo when Jackie's brother Dale decided to sell his house and eighty acres. Clark and Jackie offered Dale the Ford or the Studebaker and some cash for his place. Dale decided on the dented Ford rather than the Studebaker. By the time Clark returned from Pendleton, Jackie had moved into their new home. Later Clark bought an additional eighty acres to add to their pastureland.

Jackie was pregnant during the last move. "I was convinced that I was the first woman to ever be pregnant. I quit my teaching job and concentrated on the baby."

A few months after the move Alice Lynn, named in honor of Clark's mother, was born December 3, 1951. Eighteen months later on June 23 of 1953, their son Del Stanley was born. They nicknamed the baby "Pecos Pete" before he was born. After Del arrived, they shortened the nickname to Pake, which later became his legal name. While checking the baby, they noticed he had a birthmark on the outside of his left knee which was identical to the one Clark's mother had had on that same spot.

Clark brought Jackie and Pake home the morning of June 26, then left that afternoon to hit the rodeo circuit. He was gone for six weeks. During that time, Pake grew and changed. Clark jokingly accused Jackie of switching babies and checked the baby's knee for the birthmark.

A second daughter, Reba Nell, was born March 28, 1955. The little redhead was named Reba, after her grandmother Reba Smith and Nell after a close friend of the family.

Jackie was happy in the little house by the creek. Drawing water from the well didn't seem like a problem since she had an electric refrigerator, gas for heat, and a wringer washing machine. These were luxuries to a woman who had lived her early years using kerosene lamps, wood stoves, and washing on a rub board.

All was going well for the McEntire family. Clark was winning enough to feed them well. Meanwhile, the kids were growing and doing fine. Then came the announcement that they would have to sell their house and land. Oklahoma City was in need of a new water source and decided to build a large lake near Atoka. Several families, including the McEntires, had to relocate.

Clark bought 340 acres in Atoka County near the Chockie

settlement and built a house for his family. They lived there for thirty-two years before moving to a home near Atoka. Jackie admitted that she often got homesick for the mountains and her old home at Chockie.

The building of Atoka Lake affected some of the small rural schools. Limestone Gap School closed, forcing students to transfer to Kiowa. Changes were necessary to accommodate the consolidation. One of those changes was the expansion of the library. The superintendent asked Jackie to help with the new library. Thinking it would be a short-term thing, she agreed. As it turned out, she stayed for eleven years, keeping books and serving as clerk for the board of education.

Martha Susan (Susie) was born November 8, 1957. She was named for her maternal grandmothers, Susie Brasfield and Martha Hayhurst. Jackie had her hands full raising four children, with the oldest only five years old. Although it was difficult to manage with Clark gone most of the time, she said those early days held some of her best memories.

"When the kids were little, many nights were spent in this chair," Jackie said, rocking gently in a sturdy western-style rocker. "I held Susie in my lap, Reba sat beside me, Pake sat on one chair arm, and Alice sat on the other. We sang songs, read books, and told stories to pass the time. Those were lonely times, but golden times, and years that I wouldn't trade for anything."

The kids seemed to go from the rocking chair to about every activity they could find. They were in 4-H Club and played basketball while attending Kiowa schools. At home they were busy working on the ranch and practicing roping and barrel racing. Weekends were spent traveling to horse shows and barrel races. Jackie drove and pulled the horses.

"We were busy, no doubt about that. Pake and Alice won a total of nineteen trophies in one weekend."

Alice ran barrels and did quite well. Before retiring, she won second in the IRA national finals. Reba and Susie were small at the time Alice was going to so many rodeos. Jackie would tell them the night before a show: "The car will be leaving at four a.m. if you little girls want to go be in the backseat." They didn't mind the hour they left, but did mind being called 'little girls'.

Reba was a tough competitor, but her horse wasn't as good as the one Alice rode. Clark told her that she'd better stick with her music. As it turned out, that was good advice.

In the early years of their marriage Jackie went with Clark to rodeos. Many times they could only grab a few hours sleep, so they threw a blanket on the ground and slept. Later, when the whole family traveled, they rented a motel room.

"Our budget only allowed eight dollars for a motel room. Sometimes we had to drive a ways to find one in our price range, but we always did. It's hard to believe that a room is ten times that much today," Jackie said.

Jackie enjoyed traveling with Clark but was always getting into some kind of situation. The dented new Ford seemed to start a series of events at rodeos. When they traveled to the Denver rodeo, which was held in a coliseum, Jackie had to climb to the very top row to find a seat. She made it to the top, turned around to sit down, but fainted dead away. When she came to, a man helped her to the Red Cross station.

An announcement came over the loud speaker: "A woman has fainted in the grandstand."

Clark made the comment that it was probably Jackie. One of the cowboys walked up about that time and told Clark that he'd just seen Jackie in the Red Cross tent and asked if she might be in the family way. As it turned out, she wasn't expecting. She just wasn't accustomed to climbing that many stairs in high altitudes.

Jackie was minding her own business and enjoying visiting with her friend Pauline Kinyon at the Antlers Rodeo when they spotted another friend, Betty Simpson Woods, on the other side of the arena.

The two started walking around to visit with Betty. The announcer called: "A bull has jumped the fence!"

Someone else said: "Here he comes."

Jackie took off running. When she looked back, the bull was right behind her and gaining ground. Ted McMillan saved her by grabbing her and pulling her against the fence.

"He almost got that woman!" the announcer shared with the crowd, as the bull rushed by Jackie.

"I mostly stayed out of trouble after that," Jackie said with a chuckle.

Traveling to rodeos is fast-paced. Many times cowboys finish one show, load up and drive day and night to make the next one. It was not easy when traveling with four children, but Jackie and the kids did often travel with Clark. Pendleton, Oregon became one of their favorites. The entire community supported the rodeo.

"Businesses closed and often rodeo contestants and their families were invited to stay with local residents," Jackie recalled. "Schools brought students to the rodeo performances. It was a wonderful festive event that everyone loved"

While traveling with Clark was fun, keeping up with four kids wasn't. When Jackie tried to explain that to Clark, he just didn't understand. He was always busy getting ready to rope, so he didn't realize how hard it was to keep four little ones seated on bleachers for long periods of time. He began to understand when they took the kids to a circus, and he had to help manage them for two hours. Just keeping clothes clean and packed was an ordeal. Jackie would get home, start laundry, and pack for the next rodeo. She and Clark finally decided that it would be best for her and the kids to stay home and just go to rodeos that were close.

There were many adventures at home. Always, it seemed things went wrong as soon as the dust settled from Clark's leaving. A horse would go lame, steers would get out of the pasture, or some machinery would break down. Jackie and the kids were all good riders so any problem that could be solved on horseback was handled easily. Rattlesnakes and the railroad tracks were a different story.

Relatives worried that a train would hit one of the kids when they crossed the tracks going to the roping pen. Others wanted to build a snake-proof fence around the house. Clark didn't worry about snakes.

"The kids are never at the house," he said. "They're at the roping pen, and surely they can see a train."

One time a cattle truck had stalled on the train tracks. The driver honked the horn, until they realized something was wrong. Knowing a train was due any minute Jackie went for pliers to cut the wires and throw a switch. Vernon McCormick managed to jump-start the truck and get it off the track just in time.

Like most ropers, Clark spent much of his time at the roping pen. His father started him roping at a young age and Clark entered competition at fifteen. He won his first championship in 1947 when he was nineteen. His dream was someday to win both Pendleton, Oregon and Cheyenne, Wyoming. Not only did Clark win both, he also won the Oregon-California International Rodeo title. In 1957, 1958, and 1961 he won the Rodeo Cowboys' Steer Roping Championship. In 1988 he was inducted into the National Cowboy Hall of Fame, joining his father John who was inducted in 1984.

Clark retired from rodeo in 1973 after participating in the Pawhuska, Oklahoma steer roping. Jackie retired that same year so that they could work on the ranch together.

They agreed that rodeo had been good to them. Not only did it provide money to pay the bills, they also became part of an extended rodeo family. Clark and Jackie traveled to more than thirty states and their children were exposed to a unique way of life. The friendships they formed with other rodeo families continue today. Travel, competition, and meeting famous people gave the children confidence and a desire to excel.

Pake and Reba first sang professionally at the Cheyenne, Wyoming Frontier Days Rodeo. One of the cowboys offered Pake a quarter if he would sing. Little Reba wanted in on the action. After a bit of haggling, Everett Shaw gave her a nickel and the performance began.

The four McEntire children have done well with their lives.

"We have eleven grandchildren, four great grandchildren, and five step grandchildren," said Jackie. "Many of these youngsters rodeo, or are being influenced or fed by money earned at rodeos. We only hope that they acquire as many lasting friendships as we have."

Rodeo life has changed much since Jackie and Clark's days. Twenty-first century cowboys and cowgirls travel at a much faster pace. Many contestants fly from one show to another and enter via e-mail or cell phone. They drive big trucks and pull trailers that have living quarters built in. They have doctors and trainers on the spot and the very latest in sophisticated equipment. There are roping schools, riding schools, and videos to help individuals become tops in their field.

In the 1950's and '60's' everyone drove from one show to another, and were easily recognized by their rigs. When they pulled into the rodeo grounds, their arrival was announced before they got out of their vehicles.

Jackie laughed, recalling an outfit that was certainly easy to recognize. "Everett Shaw and John McEntire built a horse trailer for under $45. Then bought a Model-A Ford with no top for $225. Once their rig was completed, they loaded their horses and headed for Wolf Point, Montana."

"Be sure you think enough of the cowboy you marry to endure the bad times as well as the good," Jackie advised rodeo wives or women thinking of marrying a cowboy. "It's not like having a salary come in on a regular basis. You have to be patient and not gripe when he doesn't win. He feels bad enough without having his wife start in on him. In fact, don't go into the marriage planning on him winning a lot of money. It won't work out that way every time. But rodeo was good to us. It paid the grocery bill."

A nice easygoing woman, Jackie's life wasn't easy when Clark was away from home. She had to make decisions when they needed to be made. Instead of complaining and feeling sorry for herself, she made the best of her situation. With the aid of a rocking chair she helped her children feel secure and loved, and taught them skills that would help them succeed in life.

In March of 2000, Jackie and Clark celebrated their fiftieth wedding anniversary. Their children hosted a celebration for them at the National Cowboy and Western Heritage Museum in Oklahoma City, Oklahoma. It was a joy to watch a famous cowboy dance with his lifelong sweetheart.

Jackie Smith and Clark McEntire on a date (1949).

Jackie Smith standing on the back of her mount.

Jackie and Clark McEntire dancing at the National Cowboy and Western Heritage Museum in Oklahoma City, celebrating their 50th wedding anniversary (2000).

Children of Jackie and Clark McEntire entertaining at their 50th wedding anniversary. Left to right: Reba, Alice, Susie, and Pake.

Judy Goodspeed (daughter of Buck and Decie Goodspeed) with Reba McEntire (daughter of Clark and Jackie) at the McEntire's 50th wedding anniversary (2000).

VI

Donna
Casity McSpadden

DONNA thought that, after marrying rodeo announcer Clem McSpadden, her life would be a romantic adventure filled with exciting travels and interesting people.

"It was probably after the second or third show that I found rodeo life wasn't exactly as I had fantasized," Donna said. "We left home and drove to Lubbock, Texas; then from Lubbock to Coleman, Texas. We left Coleman and drove straight through to Salt Lake City, Utah. We arrived in Salt Lake City in time for the first performance of the rodeo. When Clem finished announcing the rodeo, we were more than ready for a good night's sleep.

"Being new at this game I didn't know that it was a common practice for cowboys who didn't have a room to find someone who did and bunk with them. I was a bit surprised when Carl Nafzger and two other cowboys showed up at our room, and even more surprised when Clem invited them to spend the night. My first thought was what if I need to go to the bathroom? Sure enough sometime in the early morning hours my fear became a reality. I quietly slipped out of bed and tiptoed toward the bathroom. I almost had it made when I stepped right in the middle of Carl. He let out a groan, turned over and went right back to sleep. The others were so tired they didn't even move."

Traveling from rodeo to rodeo often meant driving day and night. There wasn't time for sight seeing or long stops. Wives and kids learned to train their bladders with the fuel tank. If the driver got sleepy, he gave hints by turning on the wipers and the radio. You ate when you stopped for gas and, often, the meal was a bag of chips or a packaged sandwich.

"Cowboys thought nothing of dropping by for a bite to eat," Donna recalled. "They knew I always kept sandwich fixings and snacks in the room. I don't know how many times one of the guys needed to shower and used the last clean towel. At first I didn't know what to think, and then I realized that this is what makes rodeo life so special."

"Later, when we went to the rodeo at Wichita Falls, Texas, I had been to do the laundry and stopped by the motel office to borrow an ironing board. I returned to the room and began ironing. Clem was lying on the bed resting when Nocona Slim stuck his head into the open door. He said, 'Looks like you picked a good little woman, Clem. You've already got her taking in ironing.'"

Donna Casity was born at Cleveland, Oklahoma to C. A. and Edna Fox Casity. The second of two daughters, Donna was only twenty-three months younger than Norma.

"Norma is the smart, talented one. She does the cooking, sewing, crocheting, plays the piano, and can carry a tune. I took lessons in all of the above and flunked, but I can change the oil in the car or tractor."

The family traveled often when the girls were small. Mr. Casity was an inspector for Williams Brothers, and Ford, Bacon, and Davis, pipeline companies. He also worked heavy-duty construction. There were times when the girls attended three or four different schools in a year. Changing schools wasn't a problem for Norma and Donna. Each change was a new challenge and the girls were both excellent students.

"We thought nothing of moving. Mom made every motel room or apartment feel like home."

The Casitys were living in Spartanburg, South Carolina when Pearl Harbor was bombed. Donna remembered really liking the city. She also remembered the day her father and cousin, who was working for him, left to go to work. They turned right around and came back.

"My dad held Mom's hand and said, 'Dutch, Pearl Harbor's been bombed.'"

After Donna's cousin said he was going home, her dad said, "We're going home, too. I might can help."

When they arrived in Oklahoma, C. A. went immediately to join the army. However, years before he had broken his back while working on an oil rig, so the army rejected him. His company then sent him with a crew to Port St. Joe, Florida to secure loading tankers and barges with heavy equipment.

"Norma and I went to school in Port Saint Joe wearing our pretty dresses and cowboy boots. The other students looked at us funny, but we thought we were cute. Mom made most of our clothes, so we always dressed nice. Finally, kids began asking us how cowboy boots felt. Later in the year we put our boots away and started wearing shoes."

The time came when C. A. was being sent to different jobs, making it difficult for the family to travel with him. Edna and the girls returned to Craig County in northeastern Oklahoma to be near her parents. Later, they bought a house there and the girls attended White Oak Schools.

Donna was involved in many activities. One year she played the part of Nan in the play *Lighthouse Nan*. Her best friend, an Indian girl named Majel Dick, played Hortense Star. They did such a good job they were asked to repeat their performance.

In later years Majel suffered a brain aneurysm and was flown to Dallas, Texas, for surgery. She recovered from surgery but remained in a coma. Donna flew to Dallas to be with her friend.

"I walked into the room and just for an instant there was recognition. She did recover, but is in a wheelchair part of the time. I've gone to many stomp dances with Majel and her family. I was probably the only blonde haired, blue-eyed person there. I even danced with them. I realize now what an honor it was to be asked to dance."

By the time Donna reached high school, her dad had returned

home. When he was elected to the school board, Donna thought that made her privileged.

"A friend of mine and I skipped school and went to Ketchum to a baseball game. The next morning the superintendent called me into his office. He talked with me a bit and then told me that I was to recite *Thanatopsis* in front of the whole school the next morning, and that my parents would be sitting on the front row. Believe you me I was ready to recite the next morning."

Donna enjoyed all school activities but playing basketball was her favorite. The students were allowed to go to the gym at noon after they finished their lunch. It didn't take Donna long to swallow her lunch and get to the gym. Her number was "00" and she played forward.

The girls had responsibilities when they got home from school. For years Donna didn't realize her sister was a con artist.

"Norma would say, 'Mother I'll be glad to cook,' or 'Mother I'll clean the house.' That left me to do the outside work."

Donna really didn't mind all that much. She loved being outside operating equipment and working with her parents.

Her childhood years were happy, even though at times she was sent to cut her own switch for spankings. There were also times that she was called to the front pew in church and seated between her parents.

They were a close family. Meals were eaten together at the table. Please and thank you were expected and if you failed to say them you were asked to leave the table. Every time the church doors were open, the Casity family was there. Bible School and Sunday School parties were held at their house as well as post basketball game parties.

"Every ballgame night Mother made stew. It was much later that I realized why. She could easily add a few more potatoes and water if she needed to feed more people. Never did my parents complain that we brought too many kids home or about friends spending the night."

The family lived in a two-story house that was heated with wood or coal. The girls slept upstairs. The chimney ran through the center of their bedroom. Norma came up with the idea of each guest signing her name on a brick, plus the name of the team they played that night, the score, and the date. Donna didn't think much about it then but would love to have those bricks now.

After graduating from high school, Donna went to work for Dick Wheatley, an attorney in Vinita. Evelyn Cusick was his legal assistant and secretary. Working with Evelyn, whetted Donna's appetite for the legal world.

Donna left Dick Wheatley's office and went to work for the County Attorney, L.O. Thomas. She hadn't been working long when the director of the Department of Public Welfare offered her a job. She took the job but later realized that she preferred working for the County Attorney.

An opportunity came for Donna to work in the personnel department of Shell Oil Company in Tulsa.

"I loved it. I didn't know that people living in Rogers County, Craig County, and Tulsa County Oklahoma corresponded daily with people in the Netherlands, and everywhere else in the world. I often had phone conversations with someone at The Hague. This was the greatest geography lesson a person could get."

Donna was working for Shell Oil when Elvis Presley became popular. He was scheduled to give a concert in Tulsa. Colonel Tom Parker called Shell Oil and asked the head of personnel to pick out five girls to sit on the front row at the concert. This was called staging. Donna was one of the girls chosen.

"I wore a robin's egg blue A-line dress and matching blue heels that had little bows on top. We were real close to the stage and got a good look at the boys in the band. They were really cute and so was Elvis, but of course he knew it. After the concert, Colonel Parker invited us to stay for hamburgers and cokes. We accepted, not dreaming that Elvis would be there, but he was. All of the guys were friendly and nice. They were just good old country fellows. We all received flowers the next day. I corresponded with one of the band members for a while. Occasionally, one of his letters would have a little note added in saying: *'Hi Miss Donna. How are you?'* and it was signed *'El.'*"

Years later Elvis appeared in concert at the Lloyd Noble Center in Norman, Oklahoma. Clem got five tickets on the third row and gave them to Donna. She took her sister Norma, Norma's daughter Telia, and two friends with her.

"One of my friends, Brenda, and I each caught a scarf that was thrown during the concert. I put mine in a plastic bag and stored it among my souvenirs."

Donna loved her job with Shell Oil and was having a great time in Tulsa. She was surprised when she received a call from Court of Criminal Appeals Judge Kirksey Nix. Judge Nix needed a secretary from eastern Oklahoma. In his search he found that Donna was not only from eastern Oklahoma, she also had experience as a legal secretary. She wasn't really interested in changing jobs but asked what the pay would be. When he told her, she said she wasn't interested. Judge Nix insisted that Donna come to the Capitol and talk with him.

"When I walked into the Court of Criminal Appeals, I thought this isn't for me. The carpet was tattered and the room dark. I met Judge Nix and the other justices, Judge Brett and Judge Powell, plus assistants Don Hackler from McAlester, and Ora Dews from Chickasha. The atmosphere was very quiet which also didn't appeal to me, but when Judge Nix explained what the Court did, I became interested. I said I would go back to Tulsa and think it over. I wanted to talk with my parents and see what they thought. Judge Nix wanted me to start in two weeks. Mrs. Dews said that she knew a lady who rented apartments to the Capitol employees and there was an apartment available. I was feeling a bit pressured."

Donna talked with her parents. They felt the job might be a great opportunity for her. She was still reluctant when Judge Nix called the next day and asked if she'd made up her mind. She took the job and gave Shell two weeks notice.

"I moved into the little apartment in Oklahoma City. After working a few weeks, I absolutely fell in love with the job and working at the Capitol. I became Marshal of the Court."

Donna had been working for Judge Nix a couple of years when she met one of his business partners, the actor, John Wayne. At that time, John Wayne and Judge Nix were in the oil business together. Wayne was a frequent visitor to the office and always invited Donna to join them for dinner. She still has some of his signed notes to her. After prohibition ended, the business partners opened a liquor store and the *Big D Drive Inn*. It wasn't long before Donna became their bookkeeper.

When Wayne came for the dedication of the Cowboy Hall of Fame and Western Heritage Center, he dropped by the office first.

No one noticed that he'd left his hat. He called Donna and asked her to bring it to him. She rushed to the Hall of Fame but couldn't get the hat to him because he was sitting with a group of VIPs. The Hall wasn't quite finished and there was still scaffolding set up behind where he was sitting.

"I had to climb up the scaffolding to sneak to the back of the group. Cowboy Pink Williams, who was Lt. Governor, helped me with the climb. I got the hat to him without being seen, then climbed back down. He asked me to go to Hollywood for an acting job. I was impressed but turned the offer down. I remember him having a gift of conversation, as well as being funny and telling great stories."

One of the reasons Donna turned down a possible acting career was because she had started a monthly publication for State Capitol employees called Capitol Comments. The purpose of the publication was to keep everyone informed of what was going on at the Capitol. Each month there was a special section called the 'Capitol Cutie' that featured a woman who worked at the Capitol.

In addition to working on Capitol Comments Donna appeared on telethons with Ida B. She was especially committed to the March of Dimes. There was a 'Donna Doll' that wore a long blue dress just like the dress Donna wore on the telethon. The minimum bid for the doll was $100.

For a March of Dimes fundraiser, Donna organized a State Capitol Talent Show. The Supreme Court Justices did a barbershop quartet; Capitol janitors jitterbugged like professionals; and legislators played instruments and some even sang. Judge Nix narrated the *Old Master's Hand*; an Irish man with a beautiful tenor voice sang *Danny Boy*; and a shy girl, Joy Miller, who worked for the Department of Agriculture, sang a country song.

It so happened at this time Donna was sharing an apartment with Ruby Donceel, the mother of Chet and actor Dale Robertson. With Donna's encouragement and Dale Robertson's help, Joy Miller later became the talented country artist known as Jody Miller.

Along with working as a legal secretary, publishing a monthly newsletter, organizing talents shows and appearing on telethons, Donna also held mock trials for school children who were invited by their legislator to the Court of Criminal Appeals. Students played the parts of judges and attorneys. Donna explained things as the trial progressed.

"I didn't know the legislator who brought this particular group in, but he was very attentive and often smiled at me. When we finished the trial, I looked at him and winked. Later I received a call from the gentleman. This voice said, 'Do you like good Oklahoma beef and guitar pickin'?' I said, 'It's okay I guess.' He said, 'A group of us are going to eat and then get together and play. Would you like to go?' I said, 'I guess so.'"

The guitar picker was Clem McSpadden. They went to the Kentucky Club for dinner. Donna remembers the song *So Rare* playing on the jukebox. That date led to another. Donna enjoyed going with Clem, but she wasn't ready to settle down. She really liked going out with a group for an evening of dancing and just having fun. Clem didn't dance. Finally, Clem said, "Donna, with me it's more than infatuation."

Donna knew Clem was stable and that he was a neat guy. She hadn't been to a rodeo with him, but she'd heard him announce the rodeo at Vinita, Oklahoma.

"I think to this day that Clem has the best voice in professional rodeo. There is a natural stability and calmness when he speaks. He doesn't need to use antics or gimmicks to entertain the audience. His retention of rodeo history is amazing, especially since he can't remember my birthday or our anniversary. He can tell you how horses are bred, who rode them, and to whom the horses were sold."

When Clem and Donna married, February 11, 1962, she dedicated herself to being the consummate political and rodeo wife putting away her dreams for a time.

After the honeymoon, the couple returned to Donna's apartment for a couple of months. Clem needed to move to Rogers County to take over care of the ranch and to live in the district that he represented.

"I thought, *I'll have to quit work, and where are we going to live?* We were both working in Oklahoma City, which made it difficult to find a house in Chelsea. Clem's mother volunteered to find one for us."

When Donna walked into her new home, her mother-in-law handed her towels and said, "Donna, the windows need washing."

Clem's Aunt Helen, who had walked in behind Donna, said, "My Dear I brought some finger sandwiches and lemonade for you. Welcome to Chelsea."

Then in came Clem's Aunt Mae. She handed Donna a cut-glass compote and said, "My Dear, this has been in the McSpadden family for years, and I'm probably the only one who would give it to you. Welcome to the McSpadden family."

They moved in and on their first night the plumbing burst. A neighbor, Averd Dye, came and fixed the plumbing. Even though it was midnight, he returned home and then brought his wife, Peach, to meet them. The four of them became lifelong friends, and Clem delivered the eulogy at Averd's funeral.

Clem and Donna lived in Chelsea two years then moved to a house that was on land joining the McSpadden Ranch at Bushyhead. Donna loved living in the country.

Never one to be idle, Donna took a job as the assistant to the Superintendent of Foyil Schools. It wasn't long before she began substitute teaching in junior and senior classes. She enjoyed substituting and began looking for ways to improve the educational system.

"Foyil was a very poor area, and there wasn't a head start program. I approached Mr. Felix Gay, the superintendent, about applying for a grant for a head start program. He went to the school board and they approved the plan. Of course, I was to do all of the work but that was fine with me. I went to Stillwater where the first head start program was started and found out what I needed to do to get rolling. Then I began visiting homes getting the necessary information for the application. I filled out all of the paper work, and applied for the funds needed to start the program. We were approved."

Donna considered the head start program as one of her greatest accomplishments. Many children have benefited from her efforts.

Donna's life changed drastically in April of 1968 with the arrival of baby boy Bart McSpadden.

"That's the day I became complete," Donna said.

As Bart grew older, he and his mother went on picnics. They would pack their lunch, grab a favorite book, and walk to the creek. Bart liked to explore and was interested in everything. He traveled to rodeos with his parents and also traveled with Donna's parents. He was never any trouble, just went with the flow.

It never occurred to Donna to stay at home instead of traveling with Clem. "I thought we should be together as a family."

Clem was announcing rodeos, serving in the Oklahoma State Senate and trying to buy land. Donna worked, cared for Bart, managed the house, and in her spare time enrolled at the Oklahoma Military Academy in Claremore. Women were allowed to take academic classes. She graduated Phi Theta Kappa from OMA with a degree in Communications.

A few years after attending Oklahoma Military Academy, Donna enrolled in Tulsa University. She attended classes and worked as an Administrative Assistant over five Eastern Oklahoma Counties for the Oklahoma Crime Commission LEAA. She finished her practice teaching and was looking forward to graduating, when her physician discovered a tumor in her eye. The tumor began affecting her ability to read. Tearfully, she withdrew from school.

When a seat came open in the United States House of Representatives, Clem decided to run. He was finishing his eighteenth year as a state senator. For two of those sessions he was elected President Pro Tempore of the senate. He was ready to move ahead, even if it meant campaigning in fourteen counties.

"Of course, if that's what your husband wants to do, that's what you do," Donna said. "I prepared to hit the campaign trail."

They weren't long into the campaign when Donna started receiving threatening phone calls late at night. She was alone in the country and responsible for Bart. When the calls became more frequent, she asked Clem about moving to town.

"Clem didn't want to move. He wanted to buy more land instead of a house in town. I told him that I would feel safer in town. We started looking at houses."

They found a lovely two-story home in Chelsea, Oklahoma. Built in 1919, the house needed renovating. Donna's parents moved in to supervise the work and to keep Bart, while Clem and Donna campaigned. Later, Donna renovated several houses in Chelsea to enhance the community.

Important to Clem's campaign were groups called Cowpokes and Clementines. Cowpokes were children of friends of Clem and Donna. These little guys and girls, dressed in identical western attire, rode their horses in parades all over the district. They were an attraction everywhere they appeared.

Clementines were ladies who traveled the district, canvassing towns asking citizens to support Clem in the election. They were easily recognized by their red, white, and blue outfits. Norma, Donna's sister, was chairman of the Oklahoma statewide Clementines organization. Beverly Hough and bulldogger Bruce Hough carried the responsibilities of the Cowpokes.

Clem won the election by a large majority. Now the family needed a place to live in Washington D.C. Donna wasn't too excited about moving so far from her parents and familiar surroundings.

"Clem was going to Washington for meetings, so I told him to find a place. Then Bart and I would come up."

He located a house, and then came home to get ready for the move. A friend, Bruce Hough, and his brother-in-law, Harvey Towne, were pulling a U-Haul for them and were to leave a day before Donna, Clem, and Bart.

"The night before we were to leave--actually about two o'clock in the morning--Clem said, 'Take me to the hospital.' I start scurrying around trying to figure out what to do. We were to fly out at seven that morning. I loaded Clem, Bart, and the suitcases into the car and drove to the hospital emergency room. They took Clem to surgery and performed a hemorrhoidectomy."

Clem insisted that Donna and Bart go on without him, but she didn't want to leave him. She knew nothing about Washington D.C. Finally, they decided that she should call her eighteen-year old neighbor, Allen Dye, and ask him to accompany her. The boy's parents agreed to let him go.

Donna was exhausted from being up all night with a sick husband. It took all of her courage to board the plane without Clem and fly to a strange place.

She was surprised when she walked from the plane and a strange man asked, "Are you Mrs. McSpadden?" Her first thought was that Clem had died.

The gentleman introduced himself and told her that he was affiliated with a company located in Muskogee, Oklahoma. They had heard of her plight and sent him to help her.

"He directed us to a waiting limousine. We got in and he asked if I would like to stop and get some groceries since I had no transportation. We stopped and bought enough to get by for a few days. Then we drove up to this beautiful house. I thought, 'I'm way out of place.' The owners were vacationing in Europe and had left the house completely furnished."

The guys pulling the U-Haul arrived shortly after Donna.

"We got a big laugh at how out of place a U-Haul was in this neighborhood," Donna recalled. "Bobby and Ethel Kennedy lived across the highway."

After getting the telephone installed, Donna called to check on Clem. He was fine but needed her to set up his office. The next day she and Bart went to the Longworth Building on Capitol Hill. Peggy McBride, Clem's long time secretary was there, which was a big help.

"Five days later we went to the airport and picked up this little bent over man. Clem walked very slowly and carried a rubber donut. We had to laugh when we thought of the impression he was going to make on Capitol Hill."

To show their appreciation to the Cowpokes, Donna and Clem chartered a bus to bring them, and their parents who could come, to the Capitol. The kids were in awe of the monuments, historical sites, and the Ford Theater.

A Marriott Hotel was being constructed near the Capitol when the Cowpokes were visiting. They wanted to visit the building.

"We were allowed to go in and found that the restaurant was open. Most places cringe when thirty kids sit down for lunch. Their manners were excellent. They made such an impression that Bill Marriott sent Clem a letter complimenting the youngsters."

Donna and Bart didn't miss a thing while they were in Washington. Spare time was spent going and seeing all the sights. Bart started kindergarten in Virginia and loved going to school.

"I was asked to be a hostess for the First Lady's Luncheon at the White House. I also was a member of the Congressional Wives' Club where the members still rolled the bandages for the military. Mrs. Nixon was at the club just after President Nixon was accused of the Watergate conspiracy. I said to her, 'I'm sorry for what you and your family are enduring.' She answered, 'My dear, right shall prevail.' I thought that was a powerful sentence."

Clem's term hadn't quite ended when he decided to run for

governor of Oklahoma. The first thing he said was, "Donna you and Bart need to go home. You've got to set up some offices and get stuff lined out. I'll be in and out."

"I knew that meant mostly out because his term wasn't up and he was still announcing rodeos. Bart and I moved home and I began preparing for another campaign."

The Cowpokes and Clementines, now older, came out of retirement. Norma was appointed chairman of the Clementines. The style shows held during the congressional race would now go statewide. The women all wore navy blue dresses or slacks with white tops and red jackets. At least one woman from every county in the state was a member of the Clementines.

"We spent many hours on the road. Sometimes Clem and I borrowed a motor home but eventually, we rented a bus. It was the Greyhound type--big. I took the driver's test and became the official driver of the red, white, and blue bus. Driving the bus wasn't any sweat for me. I'd learned to drive all kinds of equipment when I was young and following Dad around."

Clem lost the election, but gained life-long friends. In 2006, during the Claremore rodeo, a Cowpokes reunion was held. "Ninety-two Cowpokes plus their families attended and informed Clem that they would saddle up again, if he needed them."

For the first time in years, the McSpaddens settled in one place like a normal family. Bart attended school at Chelsea, Clem continued announcing rodeos, and Donna became active in community affairs.

While Clem was serving in congress and running for governor, the site of the National Finals moved from Los Angeles to Oklahoma City. Clem was named general manager of the rodeo and he kept the title for eighteen years. For many years, the rodeo had operated in the red. His second year as manager Clem had it in the black.

A unique thing happened in 1974 at the National Finals Rodeo. Reba McEntire called to ask if there were any jobs she might do during the rodeo. Clem told her all positions were filled, but it would be great to have an Oklahoma ranch girl sing the National Anthem.

Reba came up for rehearsal. For some reason, she and the conductor, of the rodeo orchestra couldn't get the right key for her.

Reba went to Clem and, after explaining the problem, told him that she wasn't going to be able to sing. Clem told her to sing *a' cappella.*

Clem and Reba were asked to re-enact their 1974 performance at the NFR in Las Vegas in 2005. After Clem read his "If This Flag Could Talk" and "A Cowboy's Prayer," he informed the audience that a country girl from Oklahoma would sing the National Anthem. When Reba came to the microphone he said, "Honey, here's your ten dollars," just as he had in 1974.

Donna was concerned that everything at the Finals was geared to the cowboys. The wives and girlfriends had nothing to do all day but sit in a motel room or camper. She approached Clem with the idea of a ladies' day. He responded, "You can do something if you want to, but do not ask the RCA board for one penny. If there is any money, it should go to the contestants, so don't ask for anything. You have to find your own money to do this."

"The original NFR Ladies Day Committee consisted of Mrs. Paul Strasbaugh, June Ivory, Sharon Shoulders, Nell Shaw, Irene Harris, Liz Kesler, and me. The response was tremendous. We charged four dollars admission and had about four hundred attend. Wives or sisters of qualified contestants were asked to model. For one day they wore beautiful, stylish outfits and, often, fur coats. There was entertainment, usually from the rodeo world, and door prizes were given. We didn't make any money but Ladies Day became a tradition and is still being held in Las Vegas."

Every year, for fourteen years after the first Ladies' Day, Clem would say to Donna, "For your Christmas present I'll pay off the NFR Ladies Day."

In 1976 Clem was recruited to announce the Bicentennial Rodeo for the Cowtown Rodeo Company in Philadelphia, Pennsylvania. When Clem, Donna, and Bart drove in from Oklahoma, they saw the scaffolding and platform being built in Philadelphia for the upcoming visit of Pope Paul VI.

When the Cowtown Rodeo ended, the family toured southern Canada in route to the Calgary Stampede. Clem was the first announcer from the U.S. hired to do the Calgary Stampede and the Canadian Finals in Edmonton. The Fourth of July fell during the trip, so the McSpaddens detoured south to the U.S. city of Sault Ste. Marie, Michigan where they spent the day and night. Bart enjoyed celebrating with firecrackers and sparklers.

"Another thrill involving Canada was the selection of Clem to announce the 1988 Olympic Cup Rodeo. Just to be at the Olympics was awesome. During one performance of the Olympic Rodeo, I was honored to hold the Olympic torch just prior to the opening. I had taken small American flags, as none of our guys had thought of that. All the contestants, clowns, production people from the office got great down-filled coats with the Olympic insignia and buckles. That is, all except Clem. He, being such a gentleman, never said a word."

It was also in 1976 when Donna was elected to be a delegate to the Democratic District Convention. From there she went to the State Convention, and then on to the National Democratic Convention in New York City.

"This was awesome. Jimmy Carter of Georgia received the nomination. Not only was I thrilled to be a delegate, but I'm a darn good shopper, and that's a pretty dicey place to browse."

At home in Chelsea, Donna worked tirelessly on improvement projects. When it was announced that the small town's only library was to be closed, Donna bought the books and began looking for a building in which to house them. Dr. Ken Hoodenpyke, a local veterinarian who'd built a new clinic, offered his old clinic building to the city. The town council accepted his offer and the project moved forward. People donated their time, materials, money, and books. Several people physically worked on the project and/or donated funds. The bookshelves for the library were built by high school students in construction classes.

Another project was the Chelsea long distance telephone service. You couldn't call a neighbor without paying long distance rates. Donna decided something should be done. Because of her persistence, Senate Bill 709 authored by Senator Ted Fisher, passed and Chelsea was included in the Southern Western Bell Telephone Company's wide area call district.

While President of the Chelsea Chamber of Commerce, Donna created a work program for women on welfare. The programs provided training to help the women become self-sufficient. Within two years, every woman had entered the public workforce and was removed from the welfare rolls.

Each year Chelsea's High School graduating class was invited to the McSpadden home for a light supper followed by a reception and a known speaker. The GFWC Chelsea Delphian Review Club members served as co-hostesses. "We try to make this dinner something they will remember. The tables are set with my own china, silver, and cut glass. Host and hostesses greet and seat each guest. We have a guest speaker, usually an entertainment personality or politician. The kids are wonderful."

Another notable project was locating the inaugural ball gowns worn by Oklahoma's First Ladies. Donna belonged to the Ohoyahoma Club (Band of Red Women), composed of legislative wives. Each club member was responsible for doing a program.

Donna called Shirley Bellmon and asked about her gown. Mrs. Bellmon had made her gown and it was stored in her home. Several other dresses were stored at the State Historical Society. Donna collected as many dresses as she could then asked if they could be worn in a style show. She invited the former first ladies or their descendants to attend the show. Ohoyahoma members modeled the gowns.

Later a women's group in Oklahoma City picked up the project, and the gowns are now on display at the Oklahoma Historical Society.

In 1983 the General Federation of Women's Clubs chose Donna from among 500,000 women as "Volunteer of the Year." She was invited to Orlando, Florida for national recognition of this honor. The keynote speaker was then Vice President George Bush. Other guests included Hugh O'Brian and Melissa Gilbert.

The city of Chelsea proclaimed June 5th of 1983 "Donna McSpadden Day." On June 9th she was honored with a statewide reception at the governor's mansion with Oklahoma's First Lady, Mrs. Gorge Nigh, serving as hostess.

In 1984 Donna was one of several parents asked to accompany fourteen students from Chelsea to Europe. Her son, Bart, was one of the students. They had a wonderful time visiting Scotland, England, Germany, Austria, and France.

Donna was elected in 2005 as president of the Rodeo Historical Society of the National Cowboy Museum and Western Heritage Center. "I founded a women's group called H.A.N.D.S. (Helping A Needy Diva Survive)," Donna said. "The group helps rodeo families in need. We make monetary contributions, but always anonymously. Members stay with those who have lost loved ones or those who are ill."

Like all families, the McSpaddens had bad times. In 1979 they had a house fire and lost art, furniture, political and rodeo memorabilia in the fire, but what hurt the most was the things that Bart had made. Gone was the white paper plate with his hand traced on it, and the cigar box decorated with macaroni, and sprayed with gold paint that Donna had proudly used for her jewelry box.

Then came injuries and illness. Clem was involved in a pick-up and train collision in 1992. In 1993 Donna had eye surgery in Oklahoma City. She was expected to have 20/20 vision but when they removed the patches, she was blind. Emergency surgery was performed followed by two weeks of daily visits to the doctor. In 1994 Clem had hip replacement surgery. They spent Christmas that year at St. Francis Hospital in Tulsa, where Clem was recovering from a near fatal staph infection. Donna had back surgery in 2000 and was bedfast for thirty days.

"Clem would come to the bedroom and ask, 'Honey would you like some fried Spam and a 7-Up®?' If it hadn't been for my neighbors, church members, and sister, I would have starved. Poor guy can't operate a washing machine or a dishwasher."

Family is very important to Donna. She grew up in a home with parents who gave her love, support, and encouragement. Donna and her sister Norma were very close. They helped and depended on each other. Each had only one child.

Norma married Monte Summy. Their daughter, Telia, was a talented musician who had been a Miss Oklahoma contestant. A graduate of Oklahoma State University, Telia married Don Lewis and was a counselor in Tulsa Schools.

Bart, Donna and Clem's son, graduated from the University of the South, in Sewanee, Tennessee with a degree in Political Science. He went on to graduate from the University of Oklahoma School of Law, and later became a partner with his father in McSpadden and Associates Governmental Relations.

Bart and his wife Kate had three children: Noah, Chloe, and Tucker. Kate had been a registered nurse specializing in heart trauma, but found happiness as a stay at home Mom.

Though Bart's growing up years were busy ones Clem and

Donna always made time for him and a once a year trip for just the three of them. They took the week between Christmas and New Year's for a true get away trip. The three of them would sit down and discuss where they wanted to go and then make the arrangements. One year they decided to go to Jackson Hole, Wyoming. Clem was in charge of making arrangements. When he couldn't get tickets to Jackson Hole, he purchased tickets to London instead.

"It was a wonderful surprise and a delightful vacation."

Another wonderful vacation was when Donna and Bart took Donna's mother to Hawaii for her eightieth birthday. Mrs. Casity liked to travel and was very lonely after her husband's death. Donna planned the trip to cheer her up. For her eighty-third birthday, Donna took her to Acapulco, Mexico.

Clem McSpadden served eighteen years in the Oklahoma State Senate, two years in the United States Congress, and continued to work at the Oklahoma State Capitol as a legislative consultant. He began announcing rodeo in 1947 and quickly became the voice of rodeo. His knowledge of rodeo contestants, past and present, and their mounts is remarkable. He commentated for ABC's Wide World of Sports and later did commercials for *Atwoods Farm and Ranch Stores*, as well as the famed Oklahoma City *Cattlemen's Café*.

In 1975 Clem began the *World's Richest Roping* contest, where cowboys competed in $100,000.00 steer and calf roping events. In 1976 he built an arena at his Bushyhead ranch. Everett Shaw was his first arena director. Donna started the *Bushyhead Art Show* with well-known western and Indian artists and sculptors. She had the show in the sheds with gunny sacks on the walls and spotlights for the art work. Part of the proceeds was donated to the American Heart Association. Another portion was used to lay the groundwork for the building of the Chelsea Public Library.

"We had the best," Donna said. "In fact, we named it *Gathering of the Best*, which it was in artists, ropers, volunteers, and talent."

In 1983 Clem brought pasture roping and pasture barrel race to Oklahoma, even incorporating pasture calf roping and bulldogging. It didn't take long for pasture calf roping and bulldogging to phase out. "While Clem is busy with summer scheduling of rodeos and political meetings, I set up the roping with invitations and take entries," Donna said. "I make blackberry cobblers that are sold as a major fundraiser for the Delphian Review Club. I love to design the Bushyhead t-shirts, caps, and programs. Nell Shaw and Bart have been the t-shirt vendors at *Bart's of Bushyhead* for years."

Donna applied for the "Bushyhead Pasture Roping and Barrel Race" to be approved as one of the State's Centennial Celebrations in 2007. In compliance with the state's requirements, the Delphian Review Club implemented two years of historical recognition and preservation in the Bushyhead/Chelsea community.

Donna and Clem were at the Miami rodeo once with Sharon and Jim Shoulders, when a tobacco sponsor asked for women to volunteer for a tobacco spitting contest. Donna talked Sharon into entering. "We were the only two entries. I put a chew in my mouth and was working it around trying to get enough juice to spit. Just about the time I had a mouthful of juice someone asked me a question. I didn't know what to do with the juice so I swallowed it so I could talk. Sharon won the contest because I was so dizzy and sick I couldn't spit. I do remember Clem saying over the microphone, 'Good heavens, Jim, that's our wives.'" Sharon won the gold spittoon, but shared it with Donna by sending it to her every other year.

Donna said that she sometimes wonders what she would have done with her life if she hadn't married when she did. Governor, president, foreign ambassador, teacher, doctor, were some of the occupations that came to my mind.

In their forty-four years of marriage, Clem and Donna made lasting friendships in both the rodeo and political arenas.

"Clem continues to announce rodeos and I do volunteer work," Donna said. "He spends three or four days a week at the Capitol."

Donna stayed home in Chelsea to work in their office in the McSpadden Building. In 1929 it was a feed store and creamery, and then later a doctor's office. The McSpaddens turned it into a beautiful office filled with photos, buckles, plaques, saddles, paintings, posters and volumes of newspaper articles.

Donna McSpadden, always a kind and compassionate woman with a great sense of humor and an enthusiasm for life, touched the lives of many people and helped her husband achieve great success. To say she wore many hats would be an understatement.

"We recognize God as our strength and hope, family as support, and friends as the link to complete our life's circle. I again emphasize, Bart is more than my son. He is what made me a complete person. Nothing is greater than being a Mother. Norma is the sister everyone wants. Telia is the perfect niece," Donna said. "Clem is a good man. Can't cook or clean house, but it's pretty neat to have a husband who's ridden through life with a loose rein and is so respected. I am richly blessed."

Demonstrating American Rodeos as part of President John F. Kennedy's "Partners of America" program (1964). Front row (left to right): Mary Louise Eskew, President Cervantes, Clem McSpadden, and Donna McSpadden.

Donna presiding over a mock trial at the Court of Criminal Appeals in Oklahoma City, Oklahoma, where she worked as a secretary in the early 1960s.

Donna McSpadden and son Bart in Chelsea, Oklahoma (about 1970).

Donna McSpadden showing Oklahoma First Ladies'
Inaugural gowns that she collected while her husband
Clem was in the Oklahoma State Legislature.

Donna McSpadden entertaining women of the National Finals Rodeo Ladies Day in the Oklahoma Senate Lounge at the State Capitol (1966).

Women from H.A.N.D.S. in 2004. Donna McSpadden at the far right.

Clem and Donna McSpadden at Calgary, Alberta Canada,
where Clem announced the Rodeo Olympics (1988).

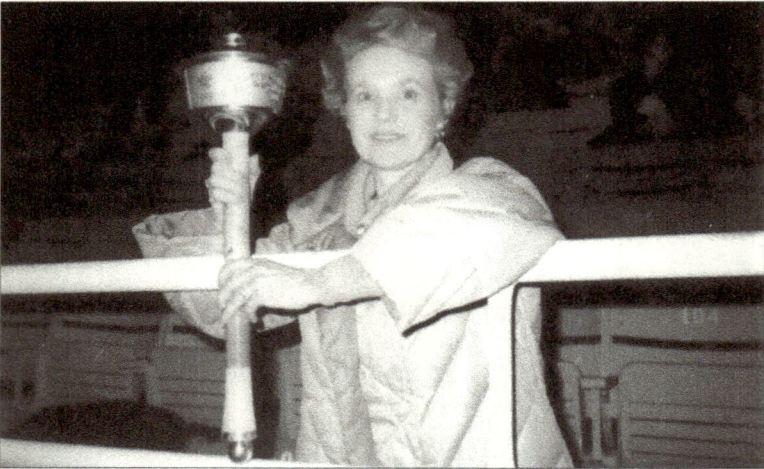

Donna McSpadden holding the Olympic Torch at the
Calgary Alberta Canada 1988 Rodeo competition.

Reba McEntire and Donna McSpadden (2006)

Clem and Donna McSpadden chosen as "Great Spirits of Oklahoma" (2003).

Bart and Kate McSpadden with their children Noah, Chloe, and Tucker in front of their home (2006).

VII

Cleo
Crouch Rude

SITTING down to visit with Cleo Rude was like putting on a favorite glove.

She was a warm and kind person with a knack for hospitality. As she talked about her husband, Ike, their children, grandchildren, and great-grandchildren, the love she expressed for them was sincere and alive.

Her remarkable story included experiences and travels most can only hope to live vicariously.

For many years, her father George Crouch put on rodeos at his ranch near Doby Springs, which was ten miles west of Buffalo, Oklahoma. Although Cleo didn't participate in rodeo competition, she was not a stranger to ranch work, often riding horseback to gather the milk cows when the hands were busy in the fields. She used her father's saddle. Since the stirrups were too long for her, she learned to ride by wrapping her feet around the fenders of the saddle.

The youngest of five children, she was always somewhat irked when her parents would first introduce her three sisters and brother, then turn to her last and say, "And this is our baby!"

When Cleo reached school age, her father bought a house in Buffalo where Mrs. Crouch and the children lived during the school year. They returned to the ranch on weekends, holidays, and summer vacations. They left the doors of the house in town unlocked while they were away but never worried that anyone would bother anything in the house.

Cleo attended school in Buffalo all twelve years except for the first semester of her freshman year. It was at this time that Mr. Crouch became ill, and Mrs. Crouch was concerned that he would need her full attention. Cleo was sent to Enid to live with her second oldest sister Neva and attend school there. Because she was so miserable, and she cried most of the time, Mrs. Crouch relented and brought her home. They returned to the house in town, and Cleo went back to school in Buffalo.

In 1936 Cleo entered a beauty contest at Woodward at the new Crystal Beach Park band shell. An Enid girl won first place; Cleo won second. Her prize was a free session at a studio in Woodward to have a photograph taken in her swimsuit. That same year, she entered the Northwest Beauty Contest held in Laverne and won first place. In 1937 the town of Buffalo chose her to represent them in a rodeo queen contest in Oklahoma City.

Opal, the oldest of the Crouch children married one of the ranch hands, Monte Reger. They became a rodeo family, traveling the circuit with a long horned steer billed as Bobby, the World Famous Educated Steer. Originally called Bob Cat Twister, the steer, which had been missed at de-horning time, began to draw much attention when it became evident that his horns were growing up instead out to the side. Mr. Crouch gave the steer to the recently married couple. Monte worked with Bobby training him to perform at rodeos. In later years, the Reger children Buddy, Virginia, and Dixie all became trick riders. Buddy also worked as a clown.

Cleo's sister Neva married Harry Carlisle, who was in the insurance business. Although they weren't directly involved with rodeo, Neva wrote a poem about Bobby the longhorn steer. Opal and Monte had it printed on souvenir postcards, which they sold at rodeos where they performed.

Her brother Glenn Crouch competed in rodeos as a calf roper. He also managed a ranch near Woodward, Oklahoma before moving to Mississippi to become a ranch foreman. In time he returned home to manage the ranch until his mother's death.

Twila, Cleo's third oldest sister married Ace Soward, a steer roper and ranch foreman. On his deathbed, George Crouch asked Ace to manage the ranch for Mrs. Crouch and the children. Ace agreed to do this, so he and Twila moved back to Doby Springs. Later Ace went into partnership with a friend in Buffalo and left the ranch. Mrs. Crouch sold the beautiful ranch house that her father had built and rented out the land.

It was soon after her father died that Cleo first met Ike.

When he and a friend stopped by on their way to a rodeo, Cleo thought he was just another cowboy. She didn't know that Ike had spotted her at a distance and asked Ace who she was. Nor did she know when Ace told him she was Twila's sister and engaged to be married, Ike had said, "Engaged don't matter; I'm gonna marry her."

That evening Cleo took more notice of Ike when he began making a nuisance of himself while she was trying to clean up the kitchen after supper. Every time she turned around, he was in her way trying to help.

The next day when she went for a swim in the stock tank, Ike borrowed a pair of swim trunks from Ace and joined her. The swim trunks were too big, but he didn't let that discourage him. Neither did the fact that he didn't have beach shoes to wear. Cowboy boots would do nicely.

By the time Ike moved to the next rodeo Cleo had begun to believe that Ike's intentions might be serious. She became convinced of this when she received a call from the stationmaster at Buffalo. "You have a telegram that you need to come in and pick up," he said.

"I can't come into town right now," she replied. "Read it to me."

"You might not want me to read it over the party line," he replied. "I'll mail it to you."

"Read it," Cleo requested.

The telegram had been sent from Pawhuska, Oklahoma, and

read: "I love you and always will. Write me in care of Chock Dyer, Bartlesville. Ike."

The next day Cleo received the telegram in the mail.

Ike promised Cleo that if she'd marry him, they'd travel all over the country, and that he'd buy her the nicest house that money could buy. Cleo accepted his proposal. They were married on November 18, 1937. Sure enough, they began traveling almost immediately after the wedding when they drove to Arizona for a rodeo. As it turned out, however, they had so much fun following the rodeo circuit they didn't even think about buying a house for several years.

At first they stayed in motels along the way, but Cleo found that this arrangement was not to her liking. Ike had to get up early to go take care of his horse. If she didn't go with him, she was stranded in the motel room until he made it back to get her.

Cleo finally grew tired of spending so much time alone so she asked Ike to buy her a tent and some camping supplies. After they started setting up camp on the rodeo grounds, life became much more pleasant for Cleo. Now she was with Ike. Soon other rodeo families put up tents and Cleo had all the company she wanted. Ike often had to go from tent to tent looking for Cleo. They only stayed in a motel when it rained or stormed.

There was little time for relaxation when they were on the road. Sometimes the Rudes had to drive day and night to make it to the next rodeo on time. Cleo began to do most of the driving so Ike could rest. Even if Ike were driving when they pulled onto the rodeo grounds, he would usually get out from behind the wheel and let Cleo back the trailer. She was a skillful driver and made the difficult task look easy.

As they traveled the rodeo circuit, they had no air conditioners, no campers, and no horse trailer with living quarters. When they found a camping spot, Ike would unload the tent and the camping gear for Cleo before going off to take care of his horse. Cleo preferred to put up the tent herself since she didn't think Ike ever stretched the canvas tight enough. Soon a small city of tents would go up, as more and more families arrived. Wives would greet one another before going to their tents to change clothes and go watch their husbands compete. Though Ike would enter any contest that involved roping, he was best known as a steer roper.

Ike and Cleo drove and pulled a horse trailer from Calgary, Canada, to Baton Rouge, to New York City, to Chicago, to Little Rock, to Oklahoma City, to Clovis, to Pendleton, Oregon, and to all points in between. Pendleton was Cleo's favorite rodeo because the residents there were so friendly and receptive, often even inviting contestants into their homes.

Many of the women were reluctant to drive in large cities, but not Cleo. She would gather up a carload of friends and away they would go to shop in Pittsburg, Providence, Washington D. C., Fort Worth, Houston, Colorado Springs, Cleveland, or wherever they took a notion to go shopping and exploring. Ike encouraged her to go and assured her that she could do anything. One city she never drove in was New York City. Once they reached Madison Square Garden and unloaded the horse, the car and trailer were parked in a storage area and left there until the rodeo was over.

Cowboys put great value on their horses and were mighty particular about who rode or hauled them. Wives secretly hoped that their husbands would never have to make a choice between them and the horses. Ike never doubted Cleo's driving ability when it came to pulling the horse trailer and, once even convinced stock contractor friend, Andy Jaurequi to let Cleo pull his horse. Andy needed Ike to help him haul his stock to Palm Springs, California, but that meant that there was no one to haul the roping horses. Ike told him that Cleo would pull the trailer and would be glad to take his horse, too. Although Andy was hesitant about letting her pull both horses, he finally agreed. Cleo calmly headed for Palm Springs, California, got there before they did, backed the trailer in, and had the horses stalled by the time the men arrived.

As protective as cowboys were of their horses, it was a surprise in 1939 in San Francisco when they agreed to let their wives ride in the parade. Since *The Treasure Island Rodeo* was held at the same time as the World's Fair, the cowboys were asked to ride down the fair's midway. Cowboys dislike riding in parades and grand entries, so for once they turned their mounts over to their wives. The women had a grand time, enjoying the parade much more than their husbands would have.

For five years Ike and Cleo traversed the country from one rodeo to another. Then one day in 1942 Cleo announced that there would be another traveler. Ike decided that they should settle down until the baby was born so they moved to Pawhuska, Oklahoma. When it was time for Billy to be born, the rodeo at Madison Square Garden in New York was being held, but Cleo told Ike that he had helped start this, so he could be there for the finish. As it turned out, after Cleo went to the hospital for the birth, it was quite some time before Billy made his appearance. By the time he was born Ike had gone back to see about things at home and missed the event anyway.

Three years later, a daughter was also born to the family. This time Ike was in Ada, Oklahoma, roping steers when Cleo went to the hospital at Woodward to have the baby. After their daughter arrived, she had her sister Opal send a telegram to Ike saying, "Cleo and Sammie Kay are fine."

Once Cleo had recuperated from Sammie's birth, the four Rudes returned to the rodeo trail. They continued to camp out until the tent eventually wore out. Instead of buying another tent, Ike bought a station wagon and took out the back seats. He then built a frame and made beds for the four of them. They slept in the station wagon and cooked in the horse trailer. When they were on the road, the mattress in the back of the station wagon made a comfortable place for the children to play and nap as they traveled along.

When Billy reached school age, the Rudes settled in Newhall, California. During the school year, Ike rodeoed on weekends when events were close to home. When summer came, and school was out, the family hit the road again.

As time went by, Sammie began to compete in barrel racing. Billy learned to rope and enjoyed roping stationary horns but didn't care much for roping in rodeos. He spent most of his free time playing baseball.

There were times when Ike wasn't able to practice his roping so he would buy a goat and bring it home. He would load up the goat, his horse, and his family and head out into the desert. The first time this happened, Cleo had no idea what was going on. Ike stopped and unloaded his horse while Cleo put the kids on a pallet nearby to play. Still not knowing what was going on, Cleo was surprised when he handed her the goat and told her to hold it. While she held the goat, he mounted his horse and built a loop in his rope. Once he was ready, he told Cleo to turn the goat loose.

He roped and tied the goat, then repeated the process again.

In all the years that Ike roped calves, steers, and team roped, he was never injured or in a serious accident. The only incident Cleo remembers happened at Clovis, New Mexico. Every year Clovis hosted a steer roping contest for the top ten steer ropers in the money standings. Each roper roped ten steers and had the opportunity to win a great deal of money.

This particular year Ike was riding a new saddle, not the Hamley saddle he had used in the past. He roped his steer, threw his trip, and turned away. When the steer hit the end of the rope, the D ring holding the cinch broke. The saddle and steer went one way, the horse another, and Ike still another. Ike wasn't hurt, just shook up a little and mad because he was out of the day's money. He never rode anything but a Hamley saddle after that.

Ike and Cleo continued to rodeo after the kids were grown and had gone their separate ways. Finally, in 1971 at the age of seventy-seven, Ike entered his last calf roping at the Matador Cowboy Reunion held in Channing, Texas. Only employees or former employees of the Matador Ranch were allowed to enter the competition. Even though Ike hadn't roped calves in a long time, he borrowed a horse and entered the roping. Cleo was frightened for him because she knew that he hadn't prepared himself for this event. Ike won the roping, however, and then retired from rodeos.

The Rudes bought a house in Mangum, Oklahoma, and Cleo soon learned to love the town and its people. They spent much of their spare time visiting friends and playing dominoes. In 1975, at the age of eighty, Ike became the first living inductee into the National Cowboy Hall of Fame. The town of Mangum honored him by naming an avenue after him.

Life was good for many years, but the time came when Ike became ill and was bedridden. One day he asked Cleo to find the swimsuit picture of herself, which she had won at the Woodward beauty contest back in 1936. Cleo found it for him, and he pinned it on the wall near his bed.

Cleo's eyes sparkle when she talks about Ike. His pictures adorn the walls of her home in Enid, Oklahoma. The hallway is designated "Ike Rude Avenue" with the street signs that the city of Mangum presented to Cleo when she moved away.

"He was good to me and the kids, and was always lots of fun,"

Cleo said. "If he ever had a worry, I never knew it. He wouldn't fight or argue with me. If I got upset about something and tried to talk to him, he would get on his horse and ride off. About an hour later, he would come back and ask if I was over my spell. If I started in again, he'd get back on his horse and ride off again. Pretty soon I'd realize I was fighting a losing battle and give up."

They had a wonderful life together, and Ike surely was a champion due in part to the feisty little woman who encouraged and helped him every step of the way.

On Cleo's bedroom wall hung a sixty-year-old framed telegram that read: "I love you and always will. Write me in care of Chock Dyer, Bartlesville. Ike."

Newlywed Cleo Rude in 1938.

Crouch home built by Cleo's grandfather near Doby
Springs, Oklahoma (about 1918). Cleo is the infant
sitting on the porch rail. Left to right: Mrs. Crouch,
Mr. Crouch and Cleo, Glen, Opal, Mrs. Crouch's father,
Twila, and Neva.

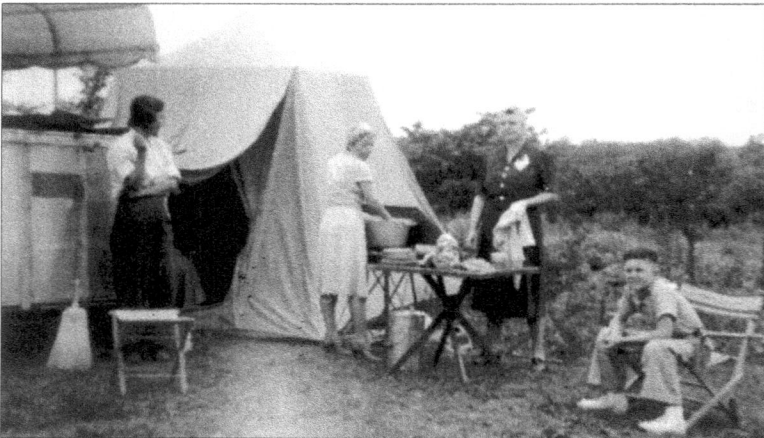

Camping on the rodeo grounds in Sidney, Iowa (1939).
Left to right: Bertha Mathews, Cleo Rude, Mrs. D. R.
Trump, and Mrs. Trump's nephew.

Ike Rude mounted on "Heel Fly" in Yuma, Arizona (1956). Standing (left to right): Billy, Sammie, Cleo.

Cleo Rude and son, Billy, at Jackie and Clark McEntire's 50th wedding anniversary party (2000).

VIII

Linda Jo
Ament Russell

"WHEN I saw the wads of money the cocktail waitresses were sticking in their pockets and compared it to what I was making doing the same job in Oklahoma, I said to myself, *Holy moley, this is the place for me.*"

Linda Ament and her mother were vacationing in Las Vegas, Nevada, when Linda made her discovery. As soon as they returned to Oklahoma Linda turned in her two weeks notice to the Hilton Hotel in Tulsa where she had worked for several years.

Not knowing a soul but fortified with a reference letter and much determination, she loaded her '74 Cadillac and drove to Las Vegas. Her former boss, Mr. Jay Chisum, had given her a wonderful recommendation. She was hired immediately.

"I had a job but no place to live. For ten days I slept in my car next to a Shell Station, which was on the Las Vegas Strip. The station restroom was nice and clean so I bathed, did my hair, and make-up there everyday before going to work. Today the Mirage

Casino has replaced that Shell Station. Finally, one of the girls I worked with rented me a room at her place."

Linda was born March 26, 1949 in Sapulpa, Oklahoma. Her father, John Thomas (Tommy) Ament, one of eleven children, was of Black Dutch ancestry. Her mother, Ollie Belle Davis, one of thirteen children, was of Creek Indian ancestry. Ollie had been married before and had two children, Wanda Jean and Gordon Earl.

Ollie worked at the City Drug as a soda jerk. Her job was to make malts, shakes, and soft drinks.

"Mama loved to tell about how she met Dad. She would always begin with 'I was at work and in comes your uncle Cleo and he has a strange man with him, whom he introduced as John Thomas Ament. I noticed right off that the fellow was poor because he wore brogan shoes, and his pants were held together with safety pins. His shirt was missing all but two buttons. The missing buttons were replaced with safety pins and pieces of wire. He had a wooden box tucked under one arm. I later learned that the box contained a shaving mug, shaving brush and a double-edged razor. Even though he was dressed like a hobo he was clean and very handsome. Later, when he asked me out I said yes, and the rest is history.'"

They hadn't been married long when Tommy was drafted into the military. He was sent to Georgia for boot camp, but was discharged because of severe asthma. He returned to Sapulpa and began working as a welder for Bagwell Steele. Ollie went to work at Wimpy's Diner. They bought a model A Ford. Tommy would drop Ollie off at the Diner every morning on his way to work.

The couple lived at a house located at 1022 South Muskogee Street in Sapulpa. Ollie's two children were grown and gone from home by the time Linda was born. Actually, Ollie's daughter Wanda was expecting her first child at the same time that Ollie was expecting Linda.

"The house we lived in wasn't much. It was made of boards with mud stuffed in between them to hold it together. A kitchen and bedroom was all there was, and they were small. The kitchen table sat outside under a big oak tree, and the bathroom was an outdoor toilet. There was no air conditioning because there was no electricity. The door frame was so low that Daddy, who was about six-feet-three, had to stoop to enter the room."

Tom and Ollie doted on their daughter and taught her the values of integrity and achievement. "Dad always said if a man's word was no good, he was no good. He lived by that motto."

One of Linda's fondest memories was of a little tricycle that her parents bought her at the Sapulpa sale barn. She had been only two or three at the time, but she rode that tricycle everywhere. Linda would ride to her aunt's house, which was several blocks away, or to her grandmother's house. They would call and report her whereabouts to her mother.

"Mama said that she knew even then that I would always be a gypsy."

Time passed and things became better for the Ament family monetarily, but there was often strife between Tom and Ollie. Tom was still working for Bagwell Steele welding and shipping oil tanks to various locations. When he passed his welder certification test, he began his own business. Linda spent most of her life around oilfield equipment. She began driving and helping her dad when she was nine years old.

When an oil well was completed and the rig torn down, all of the equipment was moved to the next location. Part of that equipment was the doghouse, which was the metal building that the roughnecks used when they were on break. These buildings were small, just four walls with benches around them and a potbellied stove in the middle.

"Dad had a Mack truck complete with a bulldog on the front that he used to move the doghouse," Linda said. "He rigged a long pole, now called a gin pole, with a wench attached to it that was raised and lowered by a cable that ran through the truck window into the gearbox.

"The doghouse had a hook welded to the top. I backed the truck up to the doghouse, and Dad attached a chain from the gin pole to the hook. Once the chain was connected, I used my foot to push a long metal stick that activated the gin pole. When the doghouse came off the ground so did the front of the truck. Once the truck sat back down, I knew that the doghouse was where it needed to be, so I stopped pushing on the stick. Dad then hooked chains from the sides of the truck onto hooks on the sides of the doghouse to keep it from swaying. Once it was secured, we went down some dirt road to the next well location. Dad drove in front and I followed him. Being tall and long legged helped, but I could barely see over the steering wheel. That's how I learned to work. I've worked all of my life and I enjoy working. I'll never quit working."

By the time Linda reached her teens her father was doing well in the oilfield business and her mother continued working at Wimpy's Diner. They could afford to make improvements to their house and to lease some land.

"Dad leased land near Bristow from a family named Cornelius. We bought some cows, and I drove the pickup out to feed them when Dad was working. Later we bought land in Bristow off old highway 66, which was the only paved road at that time."

Mr. Ament's business was thriving. He had ten employees and a rouster who helped run the crew. Wanda had moved back to Sapulpa and worked in the office for her step-dad. They had two-way radios so that they could keep in touch and know how to bill people for time spent on the job. Mrs. Ament spent a great deal of time running down parts for equipment.

Tom Ament became well known in the oilfield world. He worked for oil companies all over the state of Oklahoma. Many times he would be called out in the middle of the night and he always answered that call. This was good for business but not for his family.

As a teenager, Linda was involved in ballet, Rainbows, Campfire Girls, and took piano lessons. She spent her summers with Adena and Jess Cox. Adena and Jess owned Cox's Pinto Ranch located between Sand Springs and Sapulpa. This was a place designed for kids, and there were usually about thirty campers at a time. There were bunkhouses and a mess hall, and there were all types of activities that involved horses. One favorite activity was an all day trail ride and an overnight camp out.

"We would build a big fire and cook hamburgers and hotdogs, roast marshmallows, and then tell spooky stories. Everyone had a wonderful time. In later years I didn't go out there as much, but I would ask Mom if I could go out and spend the night. I loved Adena and them so much and enjoyed riding horses to church with her Sunday morning. We would ride three or four miles down a dirt road to church, then come back and have lunch. My parents would come and get me after lunch so I could get ready for school."

After Linda quit going to visit Adena and Jess, she missed riding and asked her dad to buy her a horse. He said she didn't need a horse. Finally, she went to her mother who was in the kitchen washing dishes.

"I said, 'Mama I want a horse, and Daddy won't let me have one.' Mama said, 'Well, you're just going to have to put your foot down. If that's what you want, you put your foot down and tell him you want a horse.'"

Linda was hesitant to pester her dad, because she knew he worked long hard hours and was tired when he came home. The longing for a horse overcame her concern, so she approached him one evening while he was eating dinner.

"I stomped my foot and announced, 'I want a horse. And if you ain't going to give me one, I'm never going to speak to you again.' To my bedroom I went and slammed the door. I heard him say to Mama, 'I guess I'm going to have to buy that kid a horse or she's never going to speak to me again.'"

He bought Linda a blood-red bay mare named Sister. She was so gentle that Linda could crawl all over and under her. Sister was a perfect babysitter. The pair roamed the country and many times came home with a litter of puppies or kittens that Linda found along the road. She wore a sweatshirt that had a drawstring and a pocket, perfect to hold puppies or kittens while she climbed back onto her horse.

"Everyday after school I raced in the back door and jerked off my dress, put on my jeans and went to get Sister," Linda said. "We made a four-mile square and arrived home just about dark. That's what I lived for."

Sister and Linda were regulars in the annual Christmas parade. Mrs. Ament would take pieces of elastic and sew bells onto it. Then she and Linda would bathe Sister, give her a good brushing, and put the bell covered elastic on her legs. Linda and her dad, who also had a horse, rode in parades with the Mounted Police. Mr Ament was a member of the organization. When Linda wasn't riding in parades, she was going to the roundup club or riding across the countryside.

"I rode Sister even after I was in high school. My friend Joyce

Gunter married young and was still in high school when her first baby was born. When I got word that she was in the hospital, I rode Sister as fast as she could go to be with my friend. I parked my horse by dropping the reins and tore through the door to the delivery room. Someone said, 'You can't go in there.' 'The hell I can't,' I replied and kept right on going."

Another good friend and riding buddy was her first cousin, Connie Darlene Davis. Connie belonged to Ollie's brother Cleo. The girls became inseparable. They rode horses summer and winter. In the summer, they also swam in Don Morse's pond.

"One summer my dad's brother came back from California to visit. He had three sons, the oldest was named Randy. Mama loaded us up and took us to Don's to swim. Connie was a good swimmer, but I wasn't all that great. Mostly we just floated around on inner tubes. Randy was all decked out in his Hawaiian swimming trunks, floating on his inner tube, and being kind of mouthy. Connie slipped out of her tube into the water then dove under and bit Randy on the foot. He started paddling real fast and screaming, 'Shark! Shark!' Connie said that she could hear him while she was under water. We never convinced him that there were no sharks in Oklahoma."

Connie and Linda helped haul hay in the summer and spent a great deal of time at the arena where the round-up club met. They tried a little rough stock riding and got bucked off, but they always had a great time together.

By the time Linda reached high school, she began to understand the problem with her parents. They fought a lot and as a youngster she had trouble concentrating because she was worried that they might kill each other. There had been shots fired and one time she came home to find the kitchen covered with flour and the skillet lid wadded into a ball.

There were times when her dad would come home with lipstick on his collar or smelling of perfume, and her mother would kick him out of the house. He would go to a motel or back to his girlfriend and stay for a few days then come back home. He loved to party and chase women. Her mother didn't party or even drink. She spent her spare time in church.

"Dad never came to my piano recitals, but he showed up briefly for horse shows. He did, however, show up quickly the day

I was hit by a laundry truck. I was in the seventh grade and had forty-five cents to go across the street for lunch at Wimpy's Diner. A couple of cars had motioned me across, but the truck driver didn't see me. He hit me and I slid quite a ways. There was blood everywhere. My sister got there first. Then Mom and Dad showed up and went with me to the hospital."

"Another time I had driven Mom's car to school. The car was a white four door '62 Chevy with a white furry cat in the rear window. When you signaled to make a turn, the cat's eyes blinked. Billy Cotton hit me on the passenger side and knocked me a winding. I was upset because I'd wrecked Mom's car. Dad walked up and said, 'Ah hell, I can get another car Jo. We can't get another kid. Go on to the hospital and get taken care of, and I'll get you another car.'"

When Linda graduated from high school, there was a big celebration. Her parents bought her a new blue '68 Camaro with racing stripes. She was the first in her family to receive a high school diploma.

Then she was off to see the world. Linda, along with Connie Davis and three of the guys they went to school with, moved to Oklahoma City. George, Connie's cat, went with them. They rented a big two-story house with enough rooms so that everyone had their own bedroom. Linda found a job working at Rocklyn's Boutique. Patti, her boss, was the stereotypical redhead. Under Patti's direction, Linda worked as a model and loved the job.

"We worked all week and then went home to visit our parents. On one of those visits I conned my mother into letting me take her television back with me. Ours had a picture but no sound. She was afraid that the television would get stolen. Sure enough someone broke into the house and stole that television. I didn't tell her for a long time."

On Linda's twenty-first birthday her parents drove to the city to take her out to dinner. Before they left to go home, they told her that they had gotten a divorce. Her response was, "It's about time."

"The only thing my parents had in common was they both liked to work, and they wanted to make Ament Trucking Company a big company, which they did. When change came to the oil business and prices hit bottom, so did Ament Trucking."

Mrs. Ament got the house on Muskogee Street. Mr. Ament

kept the property in Bristow, and Linda continued to work in Oklahoma City.

Not long after the divorce, Linda returned to Sapulpa to visit her mother. She found her on the kitchen floor unconscious. Linda called her Aunt Gerri and they took Mrs. Ament to the hospital. She was in a diabetic coma, although none of them had known she was diabetic.

Linda moved back to Sapulpa. They sold the house and most of the contents. Mrs. Ament gave several things to Wanda's oldest daughter Francis. She made enough to buy a two-bedroom mobile home and an acre of land in Chouteau. The acre joined her daughter Wanda's property.

"Dad came to Chouteau and helped us set the trailer. He dug a septic tank and made sure Mother had everything she needed. Funny that they couldn't live together but they remained friends."

Linda and Connie moved to Chouteau and lived with Mrs. Ament. Connie went to work for the Chamber of Commerce in Pryor, and Linda went to work at Fabri Cut making bedspreads. Mrs. Ament worked in Tulsa at a donut shop.

Eventually, Connie moved out but Linda stayed with her mother. Linda was still at Fabri Cut but also had a weekend job at the Lakeview Supper Club. Then she quit work at Fabri Cut and went to Beauty College.

There was a little beauty shop in Chouteau that the owner wanted to sell. She had two girls working there and they had a good business. Linda bought the shop and kept the other two beauticians.

"I kept the shop for three years, then went to work in Tulsa at the Hilton on 51st and Yale. I worked as a cocktail waitress in the nightclub. My boss was Johnny Bayouth. Big name entertainers came to the club. Lou Rawls, The Temptations, Tammy Wanette, and Loretta Lynn were some that I remember. It was a supper club, so we served a meal usually--steak, baked potato, and salad. After dinner was finished, we cleared the tables and served drinks during the show. I was rolling in dough."

Linda made from seventy to one hundred dollars a night working in Tulsa. Johnny Bayouth sold his business to Jay Chisum and Mr. Chisum brought line dancing and western music to the club.

"It was a great job, and I loved working there, but at about that time liquor by the drink failed and that really hurt business. The trip to Vegas made me realize that there was big money to be made, and I decided that I might as well get in on the action."

In order to get a job in Vegas, Linda joined the culinary union. Anyone who worked around food or drink in Vegas had to belong to that union. For several months, she worked wherever she was sent. Eventually, with the help of a woman named Ruthie, she was placed permanently at the Flamingo and worked there several years. Her salary jumped from one hundred dollars a day to three hundred a day.

Money flowed especially from men that came to the Casinos and wanted a pretty lady by their side.

"These guys were big in the business and all belonged to a club so to speak. One fellow gave me three thousand dollars every time he came to the Flamingo, and begged me to go with him. I might have been from Oklahoma, but I knew what was going on with those guys."

Linda met her first husband, Nichols Theodore Philsinger, (Nicky) at the Flamingo. Nicky worked for the state as a comptroller. The Aladdin Casino was in trouble because the owners were using money from the casino for personal expenses. This is not allowed. The money from gambling must be used to run the business. The Gaming Control Board took charge of the Aladdin and appointed Nicky to get the casino back on its feet. He stayed in control until the owners got their affairs in order and could take the casino back and run it correctly.

Prior to working for the state, Nicky had worked as a junket representative for the Hilton Corporation in Cleveland, Ohio. His family was from Cleveland and was of Hungarian and Italian decent. His connections in Cleveland reached all the way to Las Vegas.

When they married, Linda was thirty and Nicky was sixty-five. His position with the state paid well, and he had health benefits and vacation days.

"At that point I had what I thought I wanted. We spent the weekend aboard Nicky's boat on Lake Meade, afternoons were spent at the golf course, and evenings found us at Merv Griffin's. I sat at the same table with Sean Connery, Eva Gabor, and Merv

Griffin. I got to dance with Merv. We lived in a Cabana behind the Aladdin. That's where I met Frank Sinatra and Sammy Davis, Jr. I attended parties that Elvis Presley threw when he was in town. I was the happiest girl in the whole wide world."

When the Aladdin got back on its feet, Linda and Nicky went back to Cleveland where they started making trips for different companies. These official trips were called junkets. They ran junkets to Aruba, Las Vegas, and Atlantic City. On a junket to Atlantic City, Bally's Corporation approached Nicky with a business deal. Nicky and Linda bought a condo on the island of Brigantine, New Jersey. This island sits just off the tip of Atlantic City.

"I loved living on the island and having people visit. Mama came and stayed a month with me, and Connie Davis Cornelius came with her family. We sat on the patio and watched ships sail by."

Nicky and Linda lived in New Jersey for a year and then he was called back to Las Vegas. About nine months after they returned to Vegas, Tommy Ament died. Although Linda was angry with her father when he left her mother, his death completely destroyed her. He had been wonderful to her and she loved him dearly. She began drinking and taking drugs. Her life had become a nightmare.

"One afternoon Nicky came home from work and I asked him to take me to the store. Right in the middle of the grocery store he said, 'I've got something to tell you. I've found another women and her name is Rita.' My marriage was over."

Linda hit bottom and lost everything she owned before she finally realized that no one was coming to her rescue. She found a job with Reality Holding Group in Las Vegas. Now that she had an income, she began to take the steps to get out of the darkness and back to life.

"I was sick of Vegas. I was sick of men with the age-old story, 'Honey I've got buckets of money back home. Come go with me.' I wanted out, so I packed up and moved back to Oklahoma."

Two of her best friends remained on the West Coast--Connie Davis Cornelius, and Susie Michaels. Connie and her husband Phil lived in San Diego, California, and Susie lived in Las Vegas. Susie helped Linda through the terrible years of recovering from drug and alcohol abuse. When Susie called and invited Linda out for the National Finals Rodeo, Linda went.

"We went to see Ricky and the Redstreaks at the Stardust and were eyeing the cowboys. That's where I met Dan. He'd been drinking and chasing women for days and didn't look very attractive. I later found out that he had just gotten a divorce, and that he was in Vegas providing bucking stock for the rodeo. I informed him right off that I wasn't interested in a cowboy. He replied, 'I ain't no cowboy. I'm a rancher.'"

When Dan asked Linda out she accepted, but only if Susie could come also. They all went dancing the next evening, which was interesting because Dan didn't dance. The next night he asked me to the rodeo. Linda thought that they should meet in the daylight and have a good look at each other. They agreed to meet at the bucking horse sale and go to lunch.

Linda went to the sale wearing her fur coat, diamonds, high-heeled boots, and tight pants. Dan was a bit taken aback, so much so that Linda wasn't sure he recognized her. He assured her that he did and they went to lunch. Later at the rodeo, Linda and Susie sat with Dan and his parents. Dan senior kept looking at Linda, but Mrs. Russell didn't let on that she existed. When Dan left to go flank bulls, he told Linda that he would be back to get her. After the rodeo Linda, Dan, and Susie went to Sam's Town to the dance.

"We'd hung out there for years. We always knew when the rodeo was over because the mountains started coming in. That's what we called the bulldoggers. Oh we loved to look at those big handsome cowboys."

Dan and Linda were getting well acquainted by this time, kissing and hanging on each other. Things were going fine, and then it was time for Linda to fly back to Oklahoma. Dan called her everyday for thirty days. Finally, Bobbi, Dan's step-mother, took the phone bill and explained that it would be cheaper for him to move Linda to California. He asked her to come and she accepted.

"When I stepped off the plane, there was Dan and his two kids, Tanya, and Little Dan. Kids had never been in my program. I suffered through a tubal pregnancy when I was in my twenties, and I was in constant pain or had some kind of infection most of the time. When Nicky and I married, I finally found a doctor who would tie my tubes so I had it done. Now I'm looking at two cute kids that I had no idea what to do with."

Little Dan wanted to carry her duffel bag for her. He was about seven years old and not very big. The large bag, which was filled with her make-up and personal items, probably weighed thirty pounds. He was determined, and despite offers of help, managed to get the bag to the car. Linda knew she had found a helper.

Tanya was not quite as excited as Dan about Linda being there. She didn't have anything to say. If looks could kill, Linda wouldn't be here.

Linda spent two weeks with Dan and the kids. She met all of the family and then she and Dan went to Portland, Oregon, to a bull riding. He was impressed that Linda helped drive. When they got back, they went horseback riding. She knew that he was checking her out to see if she would fit in his program.

Linda knew about cows, but not on the scale that the Russell's operated. They ran the seventh largest single family owned and operated ranching company in the United States. At one time they ran thirty thousand head of mama cows and about that many sheep. There were Russell owned ranches in Idaho, Nevada, and several in California. The home ranch was located near Folsom, California. Russell Ranches, L.L.C. employed thousands. Dr. Roy Mason, the company veterinarian, flew his own plane from ranch to ranch. Pops, as Dan's father was called, kept all the ranches going. Linda liked Pops immediately.

"He was a hard worker, an honest man, and a good man. He knew how to make things work."

When Linda left to go back to Oklahoma, Dan asked if she was going home to pack her things. She didn't think he was serious. She had been home two or three weeks when he called and asked if she was coming.

"I said, 'I didn't think you meant it.' Dan replied, 'Hell yes, I meant it. Get out here.'"

Linda piled blankets, dishes, pots and pans, clothes and her dog Cha Cha into the car and headed for California. February 4, 1986, she pulled into the home ranch at Folsom. Dan, Tanya, Little Dan, Pops, Bobbi, Rex Phillips, and Mike Cavat came to greet her.

There were several houses at the ranch but all were occupied, so Dan and Linda lived in a fifth wheel trailer and married in December. One morning they sat at the tiny kitchen table and discussed their future. They decided to go with the Rodeo Company rather than raising commercial cattle.

"I told Dan if he wanted to peck poop with the chickens then I'd peck with him."

It got a little crowded in the trailer on weekends and in the summer when the kids were there. Linda had never been around children much, so having two living with her was something of a shock.

"I kept my house neat and tidy and now there were socks here and shirts there. It bumfuzzled my brain. We needed a bigger place."

Dan found a two-story house in Fulsom. It had three bedrooms, a formal dining room, and a den upstairs. A man who was moving sold them a house full of furniture for five thousand dollars. They moved into the house and lived there for twelve years.

In the spring they moved into a one hundred-year-old two-story house at the ranch in Sierra Valley, where they gathered the cattle and got them ready to ship. Once the cattle were shipped, they would go back to Folsom, pack, and go to the National Finals Rodeo. After they returned from the finals, they stayed at their house in Folsom.

Tanya never accepted Linda and made no bones about the fact that she wanted her parents back together and Linda out of the picture. Linda decided that she would try religion as a way to get Tanya to think about what she was doing.

"I told her to pray and ask for God's help, but she would just look at me. Then it got to where she would go around saying, 'God this and God that. Is that all you ever think about?' She hit me and spit on me. She turned things around and tried to make Dan believe that I was in the wrong. When that didn't work, she got the family involved. I was at my wits end with this kid."

It was about time for the Folsom Spring Rodeo. Linda had put together a package to get Dan's rodeo company going. Everyone met at the ranch to talk about the rodeo. Dan's ex-wife was at the meeting. Tanya wanted her mother Esther to come to the rodeo and be with Dan. Linda came in the back door and there was Esther. Dan came to the door to be with Linda, and Esther went on the other side of him to get out of the house. They were all commenting on how good it was to see Esther when Linda walked into the room.

"I stood and looked at them for a few minutes, and the longer I looked, the madder I got. I went in, slammed one hand on the bar, and announced, 'I'm the cow that eats the cabbage around here now. You want to be friends with her, don't invite me. Don't ask me to come here, if she's going to be here. This is it. I will not tolerate it. I wasn't here while they were married, and she ain't going to be here while I'm around. If you thought that much of her, you should have tried to help them with their marriage.' That's when Bobbi and I became best friends because she'd gone through the same thing when she married Pops.

"Out the back door I went. Here came Pops saying, 'Linda wait a minute. Now don't be leaving Danny.' I went back and asked Bobbi if I could make a phone call. I made one phone call to Las Vegas to Brenda Binion. When I got off the phone, I had a job and a place to live.

"I said, 'Y'all don't have to put up with me anymore. I've got a job.' Back to the house I went, and here come Pops and Dan. They're standing at the door of the trailer because I won't let them inside. Dan was blubbering, 'It won't happen again. I swear. My attorney said Esther and I should be friends.' I said, 'You should have tried to be friends with her before you divorced her. You aren't going to be friends on my time.'"

When the dust settled, Linda stayed with Dan. Although Dan's sisters invited Esther to family events, Linda learned to deal with those situations. When Esther fell into drug abuse for a time, Linda and Dan took the kids as much as possible.

Tanya loved her mother, and Linda had no desire to try to take her mother's place. She explained to Tanya that she would always provide a place for her to stay, food for her to eat, and that she would never lie to her. When she sat down to pay bills every month, she made out Esther's check first because she wanted the kids to have what they needed.

"If Tanya really wanted to know something, she would come to me and ask. I'd tell her as much as she needed to know. She would respond with, 'Well, maybe that's right.'"

Tanya grew up to be much like her father: stubborn, focused, and independent. She owns and operates a ranch in California. Little Dan owns and runs a rodeo company.

When Danny was fourteen, Linda and Dan bought him his own rodeo company. They bought the company from Jack Roddy, Jim Sperick, and Bob Cook and named it *Russell Rodeo Company.* Since Danny was so young, they put the company in Linda's name as his guardian. Linda and Dan have been helping Danny run his company as well as running their own company, which is called the Western Rodeo's Incorporated.

After the kids left home, Dan and Linda moved into a 4,000 square feet log house way out in the country. They sold the house in town and used the profit to fix up the new one.

"It wasn't any time until land prices went sky high, and we made a killing when we sold the house," Linda said. "We weren't happy in California. Every time we turned around, we bumped into someone. If a cow or bull got out, it caused all sorts of problems. Once a cow ventured onto a neighbor's lawn. I about fainted when she said her grass cost four thousand dollars. It was time to find some wide-open spaces."

They moved back into the fifth wheel and continued with their rodeo stock. When they went to a rodeo, they checked out ranches in various states.

"We looked at ranches in Oregon, Nevada, Idaho, and Oklahoma. We finally bought a place in Oklahoma, but the deal fell through, and I was so upset that I cried."

A guy called and told them about a ranch near Hitchita, Oklahoma. When Dan and Linda saw the three hundred-acre ranch, they knew it was the place for them. The former owner raised exotic animals and had the corrals to contain them. There were four houses on the property, an office, and several barns. The main house came with an enclosed swimming pool and a large greenhouse. They bought the ranch and in September of 2002, began moving livestock, equipment, and household goods to Oklahoma.

Dan was hauling the last load of cattle to Oklahoma when Linda received a call informing her of Pop's death. She was devastated. Knowing how close Dan was to his father she was afraid that he might harm himself, so she waited until he was safely home to tell him.

"He was upset with me, and for a while I didn't know if he would stay in Oklahoma. We hadn't even been here a year and it was a big adjustment for Dan. He was born and raised in California. Pop's death was such a blow I feared that Dan might do something foolish, but he didn't and we continued on with our plans."

When April rolled around Dan hauled stock to California to several rodeos. He called Linda while he was gone and told her that he was staying in California. She got all upset and asked him to reconsider. He laughed and told her he was teasing, and that he would be home soon.

That year and every year of their marriage since then, Dan and Linda hit the rodeo circuit in June. Dan drove a truck hauling thirty bulls. Either Little Dan or a hired hand drove a truck hauling bucking horses. Another hand hauled the tack trailer, while Linda drove a truck pulling the house trailer. From June until time for the National Finals in December, they generally made about fifty rodeos, providing some of the best bucking stock--both bulls and horses.

"We work together and in twenty-one years have spent very little time apart. I've learned not to question Dan's decisions about the animals. I had a fit one time when we were so broke we hardly had food on the table and he spent twenty thousand dollars on some bulls. He later sold one of those bulls for thirty thousand dollars. We came up with an agreement. He doesn't tell me how to run my house and I don't tell him how to load his trucks. I do most of the phone calling and meet with committees that hire stock contractors for the rodeo season. Now I might get a little carried away with a committee meeting and, if I do, Dan will give me a light nudge under the table. I'll wiggle my way out of the mess I'm about to get in."

Bids for the coming rodeo season were made every year at the National Finals in Las Vegas. One year Linda and Dan met with fifty-two rodeo committees in their suite at the Horseshoe Casino. She wined and dined the committees, offering them tickets to the Finals. Dan's work and Linda's talk kept the committees happy. The fact that they furnished some of the best bucking stock in the country didn't hurt their reputation. In addition to furnishing rodeo stock, Russell Ranch, LLC was well known for its excellent breeding program.

"Our program started with a fluke, named Pacific Bell. He was the product of one of Pop's bulls and a neighbor, Bob Barmby's, cow. Pop's bull jumped the fence and nine months later Pacific Bell was born. Bob let Pops have the calf. When the bull was three years old, he joined our bucking string. When we moved to Oklahoma, Pacific Bell came with us."

Pacific Bell became a great bucking bull and launched Western Rodeos' breeding program. He was "Bucking Bull of the Year" three years in a row from 1988-1990. In 1987 Pacific Bell was voted bucking bull of the National Finals Rodeo. Dan's nephew, Rex Phillips, suggested that they collect semen from Pacific Bell. That was years before anyone else had thought of doing such a thing with bucking stock.

When a bull dies, his semen becomes expensive. Recently, Linda sold five straws of Pacific Bell semen for $50,000.

In 1997 at St. Paul, Oregon, Bob Tallman visited with Dan and Linda about adding their name to the Rodeo Stock Registry. Bob and his wife Kristen started this registry when they began collecting semen from their own bulls. Linda and Dan were the eighth breeders to sign up with the Tallmans. Semen from the greatest bucking bulls of the last fifteen or so years can be found in this registry.

Linda explained, "Not only has semen been saved, eggs have been collected from cows and frozen. We have found that the best combination needed to produce a superior animal is called in-line breeding. That is semen from the father and an egg from his daughter. A recipient cow receives the egg and carries the baby. This process involves flushing the cow to get many eggs, then giving the recipient cows a series of shots so that they will be ready to receive the fertilized eggs. It is an expensive process but well worth it."

Linda and Dan sometimes trade heifers with other stockowners. They are extremely careful about with whom they deal and to whom they sell semen straws. Burl Ashford owner of B and A Bucking Bulls, and Rafter G Rodeo Company owned by the Gay family, are a couple of companies with which Linda has not hesitated to do business.

Trick or Treat was another great bull owned by Western Rodeos' Incorporated. He sold for $30,000 to a man from Newport Beach, California.

"He just bought the bull for an investment. He called and wanted to see him so I agreed to pick him up at the airport. I didn't know what to think when he stepped off the plane dressed in a long coat, and an Armani suit. Lord, those slippers he had on must have cost a couple of thousand."

Linda explained that they were going to a bull pasture and he might like to change clothes. He hadn't brought any other clothes. As Dan was sticking him in the feed truck, she ran and put a blanket down for him to sit on.

"He never took Trick or Treat off the ranch, and we continued to haul him for several more seasons. He is seventeen years old and is still with us."

Visiting the Russell Ranch was a delightful experience. The home ranch housed approximately two hundred bulls from ages one to fourteen or older. These bulls were separated according to age. There were twenty mama cows in a pasture across the driveway from the house. These were the recipient cows and many of the babies were the offspring of the same parents. A few horses dotted the landscape. Some were bucking mares and others were for use on the ranch. Animals on the ranch were well cared for and Linda talked about them as most mothers talk about their children.

"That bull is on a special diet because he has a delicate stomach. This guy is old and has arthritis, or this guy needs a little extra to build up his muscles. Look at that guy; he's so ornery that even the other bulls won't associate with him."

She knew the breeding of every animal and kept meticulous records. The office was a sight to behold. Plaques, pictures, trophies, posters, and all kinds of books line the walls. But the most impressive sight of all was Grasshopper's head mounted on the wall. He was one of their greatest bucking bulls and, due to good planning, one of his babies may be as great as he was.

Contestants and animals have to earn the right to perform at the National Finals Rodeo. One year, twenty-two of their bulls were selected for the Finals. Pacific Bell, Grasshopper, Trick or Treat, Copenhagen Light, Copenhagen Rocky, Roho, Oscar, Shotgun Red, and Oscar Red are just a few of the great bulls that have made Western Rodeos' Incorporated a name to be remembered.

Linda compared life to a train. "You chug along mostly going up hill, but you never stop chugging. Then one day all that work pays off. The train picks up speed and the climb becomes easier. We've chugged for years, but now our breeding program is paying off and we are selling bulls for big bucks."

Dan was happy spending the days with his livestock, and Linda enjoyed handling the breeding program and cooking. Linda did admit she looked forward to the day they could stay home and let Little Dan take over hauling to rodeos.

"What I would really like is to have Tanya and Little Dan both here on the ranch with us. Maybe someday I can have a grandbaby, or two. If Dan thinks he's broke now, just wait until I have a grandbaby to buy for."

Passionate about her work, Linda was careful to explain that their animals received the very best feed, hay, and medical attention. "If one of our bulls gets sick, we haul him to Oklahoma State University. They are wonderful."

Vivacious, gregarious, and knowledgeable, Linda Russell devoted her life to her husband and to making Russell Ranch one of the top suppliers of bucking bulls.

Dan and Linda Russell

Linda Jo Ament (age 4)

Ollie and Tommy Ament, parents of Linda Jo.

Linda Jo's brother and sister, Wanda and Gordon.

Ament family picnic near Sapulpa, Oklahoma.

Russell family ranch near Folsom, California, where
Linda and Dan lived when they were first married.

Bucking horses used on the rodeo circuit (Russell Ranch).

Crossbred cows used for raising bucking bulls for Western Rodeos LLC.

IX

Nell
Truitt Shaw

SHE grew up riding horses, playing basketball, and going to rodeos with her oldest brother.

This same brother would one day bring home a roping buddy, and her life would be drastically changed. She would go from the basketball courts of the small town of Stonewall, Oklahoma to the to Broadway plays of New York City, New York. Yet, she didn't think she had a story to tell.

Nell's family moved from Texas to Stonewall, Oklahoma in 1904. The Truitt family at that time consisted of Mr. and Mrs. Truitt, Opal, and Peggy. Jimmy (nicknamed Dick), Charlie (called Fat), Mary, and Nell were all born in Stonewall.

Mr. Truitt made a living as a livestock inspector and as the owner of a slaughterhouse. When Dick and Fat were old enough, they worked with their dad. Nell, who loved being out doors, spent most of her time riding horses and playing basketball with her friend LaNell McCoy.

Dick and Fat worked in the butcher shop and rodeoed when they could. When Mr. Truitt died in 1930, the boys bought some land north of Idabel, Oklahoma. This was open grazing country and provided a good opportunity for them to do well raising cattle. Both Dick and Fat competed in rodeos, but Dick eventually left the ranch in Fat's care to become a full-time cowboy. Both young men had taken on the responsibility of providing for their mother and younger sisters Mary and Nell. Opal had begun a teaching career by this time, and Peggy was a stenographer.

Nell, who was still small when Dick began to rodeo seriously, loved to go to rodeos with him. She gained the nickname Cowboy one day when she was riding behind Dick at a rodeo. "Who's that behind you?" one of the other contestants asked.

"That's Cowboy," Dick replied. "She builds the loops and I throw 'em."

She did not, however, get to ride with him to rodeos at Sulphur, Mangum, and Chickasha. He left home riding one horse and leading another, carrying his clothes and bedroll. He covered approximately 270 miles on this trip, and won enough money to hire a truck to haul him and his horses home. His winnings from that trip and other rodeos also enabled him to buy his first car and horse trailer.

In 1934 Dick traveled to New York City and competed at Madison Square Garden. When he returned home, he told his mother and the girls that he had made a deal to share traveling expenses next year with another guy from Oklahoma. Nell had no idea this *guy* would make such a lasting impression on her.

In early 1935 Everett Shaw arrived in Stonewall to pick up Dick. Then they drove to pick up Bob Crosby, and they all hit the rodeo trail. Between rodeos, Dick and Everett returned to Stonewall. Dick was married by this time and went to join his wife at Burrow Valley where she taught school. Everett stayed with Mrs. Truitt and the girls. During one of these stops, Everett asked Mary and Nell out to a movie. When they returned home, Nell told Mary: "Leave Everett alone, because he's mine." Mary didn't argue or attend any more movies with them.

Nell and Juanita, Dick's wife, drove to Cheyenne, Wyoming in July 1935 to meet Dick and Everett. Everett and Nell began to correspond after that, and the romance became serious. Since Nell had been attending college at Ada, Everett wanted her to finish, but she wouldn't hear of it. Her greatest wish was to be with Everett. They chose February 13, 1936 for their wedding date.

Everett wanted to get married in Ada, so Nell's relatives wouldn't chivaree them. A good friend, Louise Kemp, and Mrs. Truitt went with Nell and Everett. Everett only had $150, which he needed for entry fees at Fort Worth, so he couldn't afford a wedding ring for Nell. Louise loaned Nell her wedding band for the ceremony. The couple was greatly surprised when they returned home to find a large crowd waiting for them. H. D. Benns was Court Clerk at Ada and had called to inform all of Stonewall about the wedding. After the wedding, Everett traveled to the rodeo in Fort Worth where he won the roping event. He bought Nell a wedding ring with the winnings.

"I later learned that Everett's buddies accused him of robbing the cradle since he was ten years older than I was," Nell said. "He just laughed and told them, 'I can raise her the way I want.'" Nell never worried about the age difference, since Everett was very active and kept himself in good shape."

Nell soon joined Everett on the rodeo circuit. When they arrived in New York, the bright lights of the big city dazzled the small town Oklahoma girl. In addition, dramatic events were about to begin that year at Madison Square Garden, which would enable professional cowboys to bargain for better pay and more fair treatment. W. T. Johnson, a stock producer from Texas, ran an outstanding rodeo there. The stalls, pens, and arena were kept exceptionally clean. He was also particular about the impression the cowboys made on the New Yorkers, requiring them to wear dress slacks or chaps in the parade down Madison Avenue and in the grand entry. Although W. T. ran a good rodeo, he refused to add entry fee money to the purse, which seemed unfair to some of the cowboys.

The cowboys met with W. T. and asked that he split the entry fee with the winners. When he still refused, they told him that they would finish the rodeo but would not enter the rodeo at Boston. After considering the situation, he told them that he had decided to hold a rodeo without professional cowboys. W. T. found some contestants who would put on the show at Boston and the rodeo began. The cowboys who were on strike went to Boston and bought a section of seats for themselves and their wives. They all arrived together and sat down to watch the scabs perform. Police guarded the area and kept a watchful eye on them, expecting a disturbance. The cowboys, however, behaved like gentlemen, making their presence felt but not making any kind of unpleasant scene. Of course, the rodeo was a failure, just as they had expected.

It was from this episode that the first professional cowboys rodeo association was formed. Hugh Bennett, Herb Myers, Everett Bowman, and Everett Shaw were the voices for the cowboys.

"I was so proud of Everett for sticking to his guns and for being one of the founding fathers of the Cowboys Turtle Association," Nell said.

For many years, Everett continued to be an active voice for his fellow competitors.

Even though the strike was an unpleasant experience, New York City still became one of Nell's favorite cities. It brought adventures and opportunities of which she had never dreamed. For many years the Shaws and their good friends Jim and Barbara Snively, Royce and Myra Sewalt, and Juan and Bertha Slinas, stayed at the Belvedere Hotel when they were in New York City.

"We would meet the guys after they had finished their events at the rodeo and go to a play, a movie, or to Radio City Music Hall. We usually finished the evening eating strawberry waffles before going back to the hotel around 3:00 in the morning."

Everett enjoyed going to Broadway plays and movies, but he preferred going west to rodeos even more. After the novelty of big cities and bright lights wore off, Nell came to agree with him. She loved going to Pendleton, Oregon. The Shaws became acquainted with the Parrish family and rented rooms every year from them while at Pendleton. They found the people there exceptionally hospitable and very enthused about rodeo.

Everett and Nell stayed with Mrs. Truitt in Stonewall when they weren't traveling to rodeos. In 1939 Nell left Everett to finish the rodeo circuit alone while she awaited the birth of their baby. When Mary Sue was nine weeks old, she hit the rodeo trail with her parents.

Eventually they decided to buy a place north of Broken Bow, Oklahoma. This was an area of free range and an excellent place to run cattle. It was here that Nell had her first experience teaching school when she substituted at Battiest for a teacher who had become ill. Although she enjoyed the experience, she decided that she didn't want to make teaching a career. They returned to Stonewall in 1942 and moved back in with Mrs. Truitt. Everett's mom had died in 1935, so Mrs. Truitt became his second mother. He once told Nell, "If all mother-in-laws were like mine there wouldn't be any mother-in-law jokes." Mrs. Truitt lived with them until her death.

When Everett left after the Ada rodeo in 1941 heading for Sidney, Iowa, Nell, Mary Sue, and Mrs. Truitt decided to go to Wichita to spend some time with Peggy. They arrived about eight in the evening and were just settling down to enjoy their visit when the phone rang. It was Everett calling to ask Nell to meet him in Vinita, Oklahoma, the next afternoon at 2:00. Nell was afraid he had been hurt, but he assured her that he was okay. A little perturbed, she really didn't want to meet him because she wasn't finished visiting yet. He kept insisting that she meet him at the rodeo grounds the next day, so finally Nell agreed because she thought he was hurt and just not telling her. She decided that if he wasn't hurt she was going to be awfully mad. When Nell, Mrs. Truitt, and Mary Sue pulled into the rodeo grounds, they saw Everett under a shade tree leading a Shetland pony. He had bought the little horse in Iowa and hauled it in the backseat of John McEntire's car all the way to Vinita.

"I don't know who was happier, Everett or Mary Sue," Nell said. "She began riding with her dad on his horse when she was two-and-a-half and now she had a horse of her own. From that day on, she was with Everett constantly. If he had ever taken a step backwards he would have knocked her down."

When Mary Sue became school age, Nell put in a café across the street from the school in Stonewall. Although she ran the café for a year she wasn't happy with it. She put in a café downtown, found that more to her liking, and continued in business there for eight years. She was fortunate enough to employ dependable people, which made it possible for her to go to her favorite rodeos with Everett. Mrs. Truitt kept Mary Sue when Nell was away during the school year.

There were times when Everett would go to a rodeo without his horse. He would ride someone else's horse and pay mount money. Each cowboy had his own good horse or horses, but there were situations when someone else's horse might be better. For example, some horses did well indoors or had more endurance than others. It was to the cowboys' advantage to share horses that met their needs for a particular rodeo or matched roping. A good horse could bring in about as much money as a good cowboy. They also needed to have several horses in case something happened to one. There is nothing worse than a cowboy being afoot.

One year Everett was team roping in California and had left his steer horse, Peanuts, at home. Nell took on the responsibility of exercising Peanuts and keeping him in shape so he would be ready when Everett needed him. One day when she was exercising Peanuts, she accidentally cued the horse by touching him with her heel. Suddenly, he jumped out from under her and Nell landed hard, breaking her back. She eventually recovered from her injury but many years later would have to have back surgery.

Insisting Peanuts was not to blame, she said, "He only did what I told him."

After Nell's back injury, Everett was afraid that working in the café was too hard on her so they sold it. In 1959 they bought a package store in Stonewall. Nell found this work much easier than managing the café. She owned and operated the liquor store for twenty years.

Mary Sue and Nell were chute hands for Everett when he was home. He had an arena and steers east of Stonewall, where he practiced roping twice a day. Like any professional athlete, he had to stay in shape himself and keep his horses at their best. The results speak for themselves. He was steer-roping champion six times, and his steer horse, Peanuts, is honored on the Trail of Great Cow Ponies at the National Cowboy and Western Heritage Museum in Oklahoma City. Everett won his last championship in 1962 at Douglas, Wyoming. He beat Sonny Davis by one second and was riding Nine Bar Buck, a horse, owned by Crow Gordon.

Not only were Nell and Mary Sue chute hands they also fed the steers when Everett was gone. They bought steers in the fall, fed them during the winter, and sold them in late summer. When Everett wasn't gone to rodeos, he also traveled to Florida where he would stay three or four weeks buying roping steers for the rodeos at Cheyenne, Wyoming, and Ada, Oklahoma. In earlier years he had traveled to Old Mexico and bought cattle there.

They were a hard working family with each member doing their share but they also took time to have fun together. One of their favorite trips was to King Merritt's ranch in Federal, Wyoming. The Shaw family would go to visit the Merritts and help round up cattle for the steer roping at Laramie, Wyoming. The cattle were driven about thirty miles across the mountains to put on a rodeo. The Shaws spent most of the summer in the northern part of the United States since the climate was much cooler and there were many wonderful rodeos there.

One summer Everett, Nell, and Mary Sue traveled to the Dakotas before going to the Meritt ranch. They were in Pierre, South Dakota, on the fourth of July. It was hot, so Everett and Mary Sue went to buy ice. They brought back large blocks of ice, that had been cut from the frozen river in the winter and stored in sawdust until summer. Washing the sawdust off before they could put ice in their drinks was a new experience for them.

Nell didn't ride the cattle trail with her husband and daughter but she did work for Sonny Merritt in his western store. She also worked for him during the rodeo at Cheyenne and one year at Denver when he put up a booth at the live stock show there.

When the firemen quit holding the rodeo at Ada, Oklahoma in the 1950's, Ken and Ruth Lance bought the bleachers and started the Ada Rodeo at their place in Union Valley, located about five miles west of Stonewall. Everett talked Ken into having a PRCA rodeo, promising to help him all he could. Nell sold tickets, put up posters, and worked wherever necessary during the rodeo. She continued to work with the Lances' until 1990. Everett competed in his last roping at the Ken Lance rodeo in 1979. Their grandson Neil had gotten a permit to rope in the team roping and was to be teamed with his grandfather. They didn't win any money, but it was probably Everett's greatest thrill to rope with his grandson.

The first year the National Finals Rodeo was held in Oklahoma City, Donna McSpadden organized a Ladies Day. Nell, Irene Harris, June Ivory, Liz Kesler, Donna McSpadden, Ree Raysdale, Sharon Shoulders, and Theo Strasbaugh were hostesses. This event included a luncheon, entertainment, and a fashion show. Models for the fashion show were either wives of NFR competitors or rodeo participants, themselves. The event became a tradition and continued to be held in Las Vegas, Nevada during the National Finals.

Nell also enjoyed working at the *World's Richest Roping* and *Western Art Show,* held at Clem and Donna McSpadden's Bushyhead Ranch. She worked in the booth selling t-shirts and other souvenirs.

Mary Sue followed in her father's footsteps and in 1947 when at age nine she won Junior Rodeo Queen at Ada. Asa and Marjorie Hutchinson noticed the little girl and asked her to show their Shetland ponies for them. She went from showing the little horses to raising them. Everett was very interested in his daughter and her business ventures. Nell remembers the time Mary Sue was selling a special pony. Everett told her to call him as soon as the horse sale was over and let him know what the colt brought. Toots Mansfield and Everett were rooming together in New York City. Toots couldn't believe a Shetland would bring very much. He was floored when Mary Sue called and told her dad that the colt had brought $2,900. Mary Sue made enough money to attend Oklahoma State University at Stillwater. While in college, she was a barrel racer and a member of The Brock and Bridle Club, which was the rodeo team for the college.

Mary Sue competed in barrel racing and traveled when she wasn't in school. She was in Cheyenne, Wyoming when she met her future husband, a Kansas cowboy named Sonny Worrell. Sonny also attended Oklahoma State University and was on the college rodeo team. He became a well-known calf roper, steer roper, and bulldogger. He is an inductee in the National Cowboy and Western Heritage Museum, joining Everett and Dick.

The Worrells moved to Altoona, Kansas and had three children who also rodeoed. Daughters Beverly Taulman and Kelly Reynolds both barrel raced.

Their son Neil bought a ranch near his parents and was a steer roper. Neil won the steer roping championship in 1990 at the Lazy E Arena in Guthrie, Oklahoma.

Nell followed her grandchildren just as she did their grandfather, and even drove once in a while for Neil. She hoped that great-granddaughter Cacee Taulman and great-grandson Colby Worrell would continue the rodeo tradition.

Nell can hardly believe the difference between the early

twenty-first century rodeos today as compared to the days when Everett was a contestant. Of course, the cowboys are still superior athletes and rode well-trained horses, but many learned their skills in schools and bought horses bred and trained to be the best in their event. The roping steers and calves were bigger in the old days. Everyone moves from rodeo to rodeo so fast now there isn't time for a feeling of family to develop among the rodeo contestants. Since contestants have faster transportation available and have fewer heads of cattle to rope per rodeo, many of them are able to compete in two or three rodeos at the same time. Some cowboys have sponsors and endorse products for large sums of money.

Everett and Nell were married forty-three years. She talked about Everett with respect and great love. His death was a tremendous shock to her, and she still had trouble realizing that he was gone.

Nell was with Everett at the hospital in November 1979 when he underwent open-heart surgery. The surgery had been successful and Everett was feeling well enough to sit up and visit with their granddaughter, Beverly. Since the weather was bad, Nell wanted Beverly to go because she had to drive back to Stillwater, where she was going to college. She walked Beverly down to the lobby and then returned to the I.C.U. waiting room where she visited with a friend while she waited until she could go back in to see Everett. They heard the words "Code blue" come over the intercom and thought that it was the husband of a woman they had met earlier. He had not been doing well and was not expected to live. Nell was completely unprepared when the doctor came into the waiting room and told her that Everett had died.

Nell sums up her life with Everett in the following words: "I never went with another person after I met him. I lived for him. He was ten years older than me, but that never made any difference in our marriage. He worried about it and tried to tell me what to do, saying, 'If anything ever happened to you this is what I would do.' Now I can see he was telling me what to do. I never thought that he would die. He was always so active and energetic that it kept me hopping to keep up with him. Even when we went to the hospital for surgery, I just knew we'd be home in a week or two."

Nell felt that their marriage worked and was a happy one because of their understanding of how life must be if Everett was to succeed. There were times that Nell went with him. Other times, she might have wanted to go, but she couldn't because he was traveling with other cowboys. Wives understood that the guys traveled together sharing expenses, horses, and winnings because it benefited all involved.

After Everett's death, Nell worked for a while at the Diamond Shop in Ada. She quit working there, but quickly realized that she was not happy staying at home. She found another job in Ada at Mary Lou's Sun and Fun, and worked there for several years. Back problems prompted her to retire but she remained far from inactive. Nell would travel great distances to attend a basketball game or a rodeo and served as vice president for Legal Aid of Western Oklahoma.

A neat, soft-spoken woman, Nell's home was filled with pictures of Everett, her family, and their many friends. Along with belt buckles and plaques that bear witness to Everett's abilities and contributions to rodeo, there was a plaque honoring Nell as a trustee on the board of directors for the Rodeo Historical Society. She may be the only woman to have a brother, a husband, and a son-in-law all inducted into the National Cowboy and Western Heritage Museum.

Talking with Nell was not only a pleasure, but a lesson in rodeo history.

Nell, Everett, and Mary Sue Shaw at home in Stonewall, Oklahoma (1938).

Nell and Everett Shaw at the National Finals Rodeo in
Oklahoma City, Oklahoma (1976).

Nell Shaw and granddaughter Kelly Reynolds, standing before a painting of Everett Shaw (2004).

At the Belvedere Hotel in New York City, New York, during the Madison Square Garden Rodeo in the 1930s. Clockwise from bottom left: Everett Shaw, Juan Salinas, Royce Sewalt, Myra Sewalt, Bertha Salinas, and Nell Shaw.

X

Michelle
Smith West

A beautiful and bubbly woman, Michelle West didn't mince words as she told her life story. A *take hold and go with it* type of person, she always met challenges head on with a determination to come out on top.

She began her rodeo career when she was very young participating in the round up club and competing in the barrel racing and pole bending at play day events. Her father, Don, was a steer wrestler, and together he and Michelle traveled to local rodeos. All of her family was supportive and proud of her, especially her grandfather whom she called Poppy.

"I stayed with my grandparents most of the time. I remember Poppy would pick me up from kindergarten and I would go with him to check the cows and put out hay. If the river got out, we swam the cows out to dry land. He taught me to follow the fence line if I got lost explaining that I would come to a gate and could find my way home. I thought the sun rose and set on my Poppy, and I still feel that way today. When I was in high school and my friends were out running around, I went to Poppy's."

When her grandfather worked in the field planting or plowing, he put a saddle on the tractor for Michelle to sit on. They were best friends and she was his helper.

"I also spend lots of time with my mother, Gail, at Paul's Western Store. Mom and Poppy owned the store, so my sister and I would go there after school. We made hideouts behind the hatboxes and sometimes accidentally scared customers. Mom bought the store when Poppy retired."

Her rodeo career was going well until her horse died when she was sixteen. She couldn't afford another horse. She had a car now though, and there were lots of cute boys, so for a few years Michelle played tennis and was the typical high school student.

"When I was in the seventh grade a guy named Troy Aikman moved to Henryetta from California. He was cute and nice. We dated for about two weeks, which was typical for grade school romance. Later Troy and I were in typing class together in high school. We were very competitive, but he always beat me. How he got those big old fingers to move that fast I'll never know."

Michelle was a good student and active in singing and drama. She played the lead in the senior play and entered singing competitions. Tennis was the only sport she enjoyed, and she was good enough to make it to the state tournament one year.

"I didn't like track and basketball because you had to run too much, but I loved tennis. You could get a tan and stay in shape all at the same time."

After high school, Michelle began barrel racing again and was doing well, having qualified for the CRRA (Cowboys Regional Rodeo Association) finals. The CRRA consists of rodeos in Texas, Oklahoma, Kansas, and Missouri.

"I was barrel racing and winning and had been accepted into radiology school, when I met Terry Don West, a bull rider from Tulsa, Oklahoma. I'd never paid any attention to bull riders at rodeos. All I heard was bull riders are bad news, stay away from them. Now here was one wanting to date me."

The first time she went to watch Terry Don ride, she almost hyperventilated.

"It was a warm day in April and the rodeo was held in an

indoor arena. When Terry Don started to get on his bull, I was a nervous wreck, so nervous that I couldn't breathe. Terry Don finished his ride and tipped his hat as cocky as could be."

Her strong religious faith reinforced her ability to let go of her fears and believe that God would not put more on her than she can handle. The only thing she couldn't handle was for him to get hurt and her not be there.

Michelle soon learned that Terry Don was very competitive. They couldn't play tennis against each other without getting into a fight, so they invited other couples along and played doubles.

As the couple became more serious, Michelle stated that she didn't want to give up her barrel racing. They discussed their future in rodeo and Terry Don explained that since she had entry fees to pay, a horse to feed, and needed gas to haul him, she would have to win eighty-five percent of the time to pay for her expenses. All he needed was his bull rope and his entry fee. Rough stock riders didn't like to fool with hauling horses for timed events. It was all a business to him and Michelle had never thought of it that way. She competed more for the love it than the money.

"My family always supported me win or lose. Here was a guy telling me that winning was what it was all about, and if you couldn't win you shouldn't be competing. I married him anyway," Michelle said. "We went to the CRRA finals and two of Terry Don's cousins had also qualified for the finals. Well as luck would have it my horse came up lame and I didn't do well, but Terry Don and both cousins won first in the average. I wasn't sure that I fit in with this family."

The young couple began married life in a mobile home that Terry bought with the money he received from selling six bulls. They had no furniture except for the bedroom suite that Michelle brought from home and a set of bar stools a relative gave them. There was no checking account and just one vehicle.

Terry and Michelle were winning just enough to get by, and then Terry pulled a groin muscle. He couldn't ride for months. They were so broke they couldn't even put groceries on the table.

"Boy, those days were hard," Michelle said. "My Poppy would come by and leave us meat from a beef he'd butchered. He'd tell us that a calf died, but I knew nobody lost that many calves. My mom and her husband Dick took us out to dinner a lot. We lived from week to week hoping one of us would win enough to get by. We were at a show one weekend when Terry drew a rank bull and got his face crushed. I panicked when I saw so much blood. There was even blood running out his ears. I thought that he was going to die and I knew I couldn't handle that. When we finally got him to the emergency room the doctor came out and said that Terry needed surgery. We didn't have the three thousand dollars required for the surgery. His head was swollen badly and he was in a lot of pain. Poppy loaned us the money so that Terry could have surgery."

Michelle stayed back when Terry Don got hurt because she didn't want to embarrass him. Later he asked where she was, and she explained that she was just in the background.

"I want you there," he had said. "And make sure they don't cut my britches off in front of everybody."

From then on Michelle was there if something happened and, over the years, there were many trips to the emergency room.

"I always managed to be strong and in control when there was an accident, but after I knew that Terry was going to make it I fell apart."

Realizing that they weren't winning enough to get ahead, they signed on with a construction company and learned to tie re-bar and pour concrete. Their first check was $84.00.

"We sang *Don't Worry Be Happy* a lot while we smoothed out wet concrete. Then we started figuring how many hours we had to work at minimum wage to make what we could make in one weekend at a rodeo."

The decision was made for them when Terry Don entered a jackpot the next weekend and won two hundred forty dollars. Michelle wasn't doing as well with her barrel racing and Terry Don said that she needed a different horse. The gray mare they found cost several thousand dollars. They mortgaged their mobile home and seven acres to buy her.

Michelle liked her new horse and began winning most of the rodeos she entered. She made it to the IRA finals twice, was Southern Region Circuit Champion, and qualified twice for the TPRA (Texas Professional Rodeo Association), the CRA (Central Rodeo Association Finals), the CRRA (Cowboys Regional Association Finals), and the NARCA finals which are the top two from each association.

Terry Don was also doing well in the bull riding, but the pair were not making the big shows and therefore not making big bucks.

The turning point came when they rented a room at the Colonial Motel in Henryetta, so they could watch the National Finals Rodeo. While watching the bull riding Terry commented, "You know I could be there."

Michelle thought about what he said and made the decision to sell her horse and devote her time to helping Terry Don with his career. He was good and everyone knew it so he needed to advance, which meant traveling.

"I didn't want him to look back and think that I held him back. My mare was twelve years old, but still in good shape. I decided now is a good time to sell her, so I did. I had done well on her for two years and sold her for twenty-five thousand dollars."

Terry had tried to go RCA a couple of times. At that time you got put in slack a lot and they didn't pay day money. There were many men trying to go professional. Many bull riders would enter the smaller rodeos, but only about fifteen would ride in the main performances. The rest rode in what is called the slack. Most of the bulls in the slack weren't good enough to score well on. But if you happened to draw a good one, you might make it to the final performance.

Lane Frost told Terry Don that he needed to get in the truck with him, Jim Sharp, and Tuff Hedeman to make more bull ridings. Lane and Terry Don had competed in high school rodeos and were good friends. Terry didn't like hauling with a bunch of guys, so he didn't go with Lane and Tuff.

"If you need to go with them," Michelle told Don, "I'm willing for you to do that if that's what it takes."

When Michelle sold her horse, she thought that they would never see another poor day. They won the circuit finals and went to Pocatello, Idaho, to the Dodge Circuit Finals. Terry didn't draw well, and didn't win any money.

"We were back at square one and not sure what to do when the phone rang. It was our son Chance who was at home with my grandparents. He said, 'Some Bulls Only guy called.' We got our break and that's how we got where we are today."

Terry Don was invited to ride for the *Bull Riders Only Series* and his first show was to be held in Lakeside, California. He didn't want to go because they only had six hundred dollars. Michelle insisted that he not miss this opportunity. He flew to Denver and had a lay over, got snowed in, and couldn't get out. He couldn't rent a car because he didn't have a credit card, so he paid ninety dollars for a shuttle bus. When he got to the gate, they didn't believe he was a cowboy even though he had his chaps and bull rope with him. He managed to convince security to let him in and then found out that they had turned his bull out even though Michelle had called several times telling them that he was trying to get there.

Terry Don didn't think they would give him another chance, but Michelle convinced him to explain to them again what had happened. When he called, they invited him to the next bull riding that was to be held in California.

"We only had three hundred dollars. Terry Don didn't want to spend all of our money, but I insisted that he make the show. We figured how much he would need for a motel and meals, and then bought his plane ticket."

He made it on time, rode his bulls, and came home with ten thousand dollars. That was the turning point in his career. From 1994 until 2006, he was one of the top bull riders in the world.

His journey has not been easy. Over the years he had groin pulls, a broken jaw, had his face crushed several times, four concussions, a punctured lung, a dislocated elbow, cracked ribs, numerous knee surgeries, and shoulder surgery. In 1997 he took the year off to recuperate and give his body a rest.

The punctured lung was the result of getting on the world's toughest bull, Bodacious, at a rodeo in Houston, Texas. Few riders had made it eight seconds on "Bo." He was a big bull, two thousand pounds, but was very agile and had the reputation for getting rid of cowboys. He had a high vertical jump and could twist and roll with the best. Cowboys studied the bulls and Bo studied cowboys. He learned to throw the rider forward as he threw his big head back. Many riders were knocked unconscious, had their face crushed, or like Terry Don suffered a punctured lung. Later in San Antonio Terry Don drew Bo again. This time he rode Bo, won the show and a Bob Berg championship buckle. That was the last time the bull was ridden. The big bull was retired later that same year at the National Finals Rodeo, when he got so bad that riders turned him out rather than get on him.

Another bull that had given Terry Don trouble was Grasshopper, who had bucked him off three times. Terry Don drew him at the Bull Riders Only Finals in Denver. When his score came up and wasn't good enough for him to win the championship, the crowd went crazy.

"I thought there was going to be a riot. The people at Denver loved Terry Don and they thought he should have won."

The good thing about being a rough stock rider is it is easy to travel. Bull riders and bronc riders don't carry a lot of equipment, or need a horse, so they can fly from rodeo to rodeo.

"I enjoyed the PBR because we could fly out on Friday, stay the weekend and fly back home on Sunday. There were twenty events and we knew where they were going to be held. Terry Don could win as much as $200,000.00 at just those events. We had the rest of the week at home with sons Chance and Trey Don. We drove to some shows and the boys went with us, but flying was a lot easier."

In 2001 Terry Don was scheduled to ride but couldn't get a flight because of the tragic events of 9/11. He called and told them he couldn't make it, and they voted to kick him out of the PBR. Later, when he challenged their decision, they stuck to it saying that he hadn't called. Michelle had the phone bills showing the calls that were made. They settled out of court, and Terry was suspended from the PBR.

Michelle was business manager, travel agent, friend, and many times a nurse for Terry Don. He wanted her with him. He didn't drink, party, or gamble. Between performances, he went to the room and rested so he would be ready for the next go round.

In 1995 Terry Don was reserve champion of the PRCA (Professional Rodeo Cowboy Association). In 1996 he won the PRCA world championship title, at the National Rodeo Finals held in Las Vegas, Nevada. He qualified for the National Finals again in 2003, for the Pace Picante Series four times, was first in the world in 2003, and for one season earned the season record of $286,000.00.

Like all great athletes, Terry Don had a fan club. He was a star.

Television made him a household name. He made appearances on late night shows and rubbed elbows with the rich and famous. This was a different world for him, and he changed.

"I couldn't figure out what was going on with him, but I didn't like it. He was riding for a million dollars and got bucked off. He was mad and I asked what was wrong. He said, 'I don't buck off.' I gave him a good talking to and reminded him of some of the basics he'd forgotten. I think what really sunk in was when I asked him who had won the world title five years earlier. He didn't remember, so I said, 'There you go! Get over it.' He came back to earth after that."

Michelle loved the winter circuit because those shows were held in Houston, San Antonio, and Baton Rouge. The weather was good, people were wonderful, and food was delicious. She also enjoyed their trips to Australia, Brazil, Canada, and Mexico for bull ridings there. They actually went to Puerto Rico for a vacation, which she loved.

By age forty Terry Don stayed close to home conducting bull riding schools, cutting hay, and running cattle. He wouldn't say for sure that he is retired because he might want to try for Freckles Brown's record, who was the oldest man to win the bull riding championship. He does admit that it takes a little longer to recover from an injury now, and that hitting the ground isn't much fun.

There have been bad times that were hard to deal with. Lane Frost was killed when a bull stepped on him at Cheyenne. Good friend Jerome Davis was left a paraplegic after being bucked off a bull at Fort Worth. Tuff hit the ground at Odessa and couldn't move for several minutes. Another bull rider was stepped on but got up and walked out of the arena. He later died from a ruptured spleen.

Her son, Chance, chose not to bull ride, although he did try it a few times. Michelle knew his heart wasn't in it and that he really wanted to rope calves.

"I explained to him that bull riding was something you had to love. It had to be the most important thing in the world to you or you couldn't do it. It can't be a hobby, so you decide what you want to do."

Chance chose calf roping. Michelle hauled him to high school shows and he won a saddle. In high school he was a good football player and wrestler. His favorite hobbies were hunting and fishing.

"He moved into one of our rent houses after graduating and finding a job. Terry Don didn't want to charge him rent, but I said he should learn responsibility. He pays his rent every month and takes care of his other bills. He's a really good kid, and we're proud of him," Michelle said.

Trey, their youngest son, began talking about riding when he was two and his dad was bucked off at a show. Trey patted him on the arm and told him, "Don't worry; when I get big I'll ride those old bulls and give you all the money."

"I don't know what upset Terry Don more, bucking off or thinking about Trey riding."

Terry Don and Michelle were at a cattle auction and she spotted a small steer that had twisted horns. She asked Terry Don to buy him so she could make a pet out of him. He didn't want the funny looking animal, so she bid on him and took him home. Little Eddy became part of the family.

When Trey was four, he wanted to ride Eddy. This time Michelle told Chance not to walk beside the steer and hold onto Trey. The little steer didn't go far before Trey hit the dirt. He cried and said that Eddy hurt his back. Five years later at age nine, Trey was ready to try again, so Terry Don found some Holstein steers to use for practice.

"I don't think either of us want him to ride, but if that's his passion we will help him be the best."

Although Terry Don could ignore people's comments, Michelle was the first to defend her husband.

"He never says anything bad about anyone, and I'd best not hear anything bad said about him," Michelle said. "He is a nice, quiet guy."

The couple went from a mortgaged mobile home and seven acres to a lovely home on a ranch. The beautiful interior was filled with trophies, buckles, and photos collected over the years by both Terry Don and Michelle.

Michelle Smith (age 3)

Michelle Smith as Roundup Club Rodeo Princess at Henryetta, Oklahoma (about 1970).

Michelle West clearing the last barrel and heading home.

West family (left to right): Terry Don holding Trey, Michelle, and Chance.

XI

Cassie
Loegel Whitfield

CASSIE Loegel passed the rodeo arena everyday as she walked to and from El Capitan High School in Lakeside, California. One day there was a rodeo in progress, so she bought a ticket.

"I sat on the front row of the bleachers and watched every event. Even though I had seen professional baseball and football games, they didn't compare to rodeo."

Cassie was born and raised in La Mesa, California, which is in East County San Diego. She was the middle child and only daughter of Sally and Ray Loegel. The first twelve years of life were happy ones spent with her family on camping trips and having the traditional family gatherings.

"Holidays and camping we all got together, aunts, uncles, and cousins, for a big meal and socializing. I loved those times."

Another happy time was when the family moved to the mountains. Now she could have animals and one of those animals was a horse named Tabitha.

"We had the best of both worlds: living in the mountains in the Alpine community but able to be at the beach in thirty minutes."

Cassie rode when one of her parents was with her. She wasn't allowed to ride alone. Only with her dad could she gallop around the countryside. It was a good life, but that ended when her parents divorced.

Mr. Loegel moved to Nebraska to start a new business. Mrs. Loegel, Cassie and the boys moved to a smaller house in Dehesa Valley. While living in the new place, Cassie began riding alone. She never learned to saddle Tabby, so she rode bareback. Tabby became her best friend and confidant. This was not an easy time for the teenager. Her mother was working and dealing with the divorce. Her dad, even though supportive, was busy trying to get his business started. The one constant in her life was Tabby.

"Mother knew how much Tabby meant to me, so she made arrangements to board her at the Lazy F Ranch. In the summer, Mom would drop me off at the ranch on her way to work. I spent the day riding."

Many times Cassie spent the night at the ranch. She became friends with Tammy Free, the rancher's daughter, and loved staying with her. Tammy was a barrel racer, so Cassie and Tabby gave it a try. Cassie ran barrels riding a bareback pad, which was a real test of her equestrian skills.

"The day came when Mother couldn't afford to board Tabby anymore. When she told me, I went to Mr. Free and asked if I could muck stalls to pay for Tabby's board. He agreed to let me work. I managed to keep her there until we moved into an apartment in Lakeside."

The move meant that Cassie couldn't work at the stable anymore. A friend agreed to take Tabby to his place in Alpine. Cassie was in school and didn't get to ride often, but Tabby was still in her life. The man who had Tabby started dating a woman whose son was interested in team roping. He traded Tabby for a rope horse without Cassie's or her mother's consent. Cassie never saw her beautiful red-roan mare again.

"I had never seen my mom so mad before. She was furious that he had traded Tabby."

The move to the apartment meant many changes. Rick, Cassie's older brother, joined the Air Force, and her younger brother, Kevin, moved to Nebraska with his dad. Cassie's mother worked as an OBGYN nurse. At sixteen, Cassie went to work at TG&Y.

"I had many jobs during my high school years. Even though I loved sports, I couldn't participate because of my work schedule. I did go out for volleyball one year and made the team. They were always having car washes and fund-raisers after school and on weekends. I couldn't attend those events so felt I should drop out."

While still in high school, Cassie entered the Miss Lakeside pageant near San Diego, California and won 2nd Runner-Up. She entered again after high school. Although she still did not win that time, Cassie met Karen Ransweiler, who was the pageant choreographer and a contestant in the Miss Rodeo pageant.

In 1993, with Karen's help, Cassie competed in the Miss Rodeo Lakeside competition and won. That same year, Karen won the Miss Rodeo U.S.A. pageant held at the National IRA Finals in Oklahoma City, Oklahoma.

"Rodeo seemed to fit me," Cassie said. "I loved the music, the clothes, and the action."

Karen advised Cassie and even loaned her a horse to ride. Cassie didn't place, but she impressed the pageant director enough that she asked her to try again the next year. To learn more about rodeo and the queen competition she joined the local rodeo association.

Cassie learned as she practiced for the 1994 queen contest. The queen contest involved more than riding a horse. A committee asked questions about tack and caring for your horse. You had to be personable, articulate and willing to travel to different functions representing your club.

"For the first time in my life I was confident. I was totally prepared and riding a good horse. I won the pageant. Since Lakeside was IPRA sanctioned I could compete for the national title in Oklahoma City at the IRA Finals."

Little did she know that the buckle she won in the queen competition would play a part in meeting her future husband.

"My parents never talked about college so I really didn't think about going until the kids at school started talking about tests they needed to take. Actually, I planned to marry after graduation, but that didn't work out. Thankfully, I had taken my tests while in high school and began going to a community college. To pay my way I worked two and sometimes three jobs."

Cassie continued to work and go to college until 1996. She was living alone in an apartment in Lakeside when she met a cowboy at a rodeo. They began dating and he took her to meet his family in Alabama. After meeting his family and enjoying her visit, Cassie believed that this might work. He insisted she was the one for him and that he wanted her to move to Alabama. She also believed that he would call, as he said he would, and let her know when she should come to join him.

"I was certain that he would call. So certain that I gave up my apartment, told the post office of my upcoming move, and began to pack. He didn't call. I called his family. They hadn't heard from him either."

She was unsettled and decided that a change might be good. Oklahoma came to mind.

"I picked Oklahoma because I liked it when I was there for the pageant. Another reason was the restaurant I worked for had a chain in Tulsa. My boss got everything worked out for me. Dad agreed to meet me and help me find a place to live."

With her dad's help, Cassie found an apartment near her work. She lived in Tulsa for six months. Then the guy from Alabama popped back into her life. They started dating again and she moved to Alabama.

"I lived in Alabama about six months. I couldn't find a job, and the relationship was rocky. I called my dad. He asked if I would like to work for him."

When Mr. Loegel explained that he needed someone to travel and introduce his customers to a new internet program, Cassie agreed to take the job. His company bought and sold parts and heavy equipment, most of which could be done through his network. Cassie was hired to visit his customers and show them the internet program.

"I traveled all over the place. Kentucky was a challenge because I had to find some backwoods places. Dad would say, 'Use the map to get there, then get on the phone and get directions to the office.' Some places didn't know about the Internet, but I helped them get up to date."

When she finished in Kentucky, she went to Texas. Michelle,

one of her friends from high school, married John Attebury from Spring, Texas. They met when John was stationed at the naval base in San Diego. When Cassie contacted Michelle, the Atteburys invited her to stay with them.

"I happened to be there when the National Finals Rodeo was being televised every evening. John and I stayed up late watching the rodeo. The calf roping was awesome. It seemed every performance there was a record broken. One of the top contenders was an African American cowboy named Fred Whitfield. He didn't win the championship, but he did win the average."

As Christmas neared, Cassie still wasn't sure what she was going to do. She knew that she didn't want to stay in Alabama, but she was undecided where to relocate. Her questions about her future were semi answered one evening when Michelle talked her into going out with her and a friend.

"I wasn't crazy about going. I finally agreed to go, but didn't do any fixing up; just wore jeans, a t-shirt, and very little makeup. Meeting a man was the last thing on my mind."

During the course of the evening, Cassie left the club to take something to the car. It started pouring down rain, so she sat in the car for about fifteen minutes. Finally, she decided that it wasn't going to slack up, so she made a dash for the door.

"I got soaked, and when I went back to where we'd been sitting, my friends were gone. Looking around I spotted them with a group of cowboys. I made my way to them and knew immediately that the handsome black cowboy was Fred Whitfield. I'd seen him everyday for ten days on television."

Having worked in a restaurant for many years, Cassie knew how arrogant super athletes were sometimes. She was determined not to appear star struck when she joined the group. Introductions were made and Fred introduced himself as Brad. Cassie went along with the ploy. Then Fred noticed the buckle she was wearing and knew that she was familiar with rodeo. He told her his name and that he was a calf roper.

"We shared a fun evening; and when I left, Fred gave me his phone number. I was impressed with his manners and how neatly he was dressed. He mentioned that he was roping at Katy, Texas, the next day and invited us to come to the jackpot. We went but missed the calf roping because my friend was late getting off work.

I did find Fred. He gave us directions to his house so we dropped by for a visit. I thought that he was the kind of guy that I could be friends with."

Michelle and John left for the Christmas Holidays, so Cassie was alone. She knew she didn't want to continue living in Alabama, but wasn't sure that she wanted to move back to San Diego. Depressed and a long way from family, Cassie was thrilled when Fred asked her out for dinner Christmas Eve. He came for her again Christmas afternoon and they enjoyed the day together.

"Fred gave me a special gift for Christmas, a gold and diamond bracelet. A huge surprise for me. At the time I wasn't used to getting nice things."

Cassie went to Alabama after Christmas to take care of some business, and then returned to Texas to work. Fred invited her to go with him to Waco for the circuit finals. They celebrated New Years Eve in Waco.

"My birthday rolled around while we were at the rodeo. Fred surprised me with a birthday cake and balloons. He was very thoughtful and giving which was a new experience for me."

After the rodeo, Cassie went back to John and Michelle's. They suggested that she rent a room from them. Cassie moved in with the Atteburys, continued to work for her dad, and started dating Fred. Cassie explained to him about the situation she had just gotten out of and that she didn't want a serious relationship at this time. He didn't pressure her.

Things were going well in Texas, so Cassie decided to return to Alabama and get her belongings. Her plans were to rent a U-Haul Truck and drive back to Texas. While she was packing, Fred called to see if she needed help. She told him she could use a hand loading the truck and driving back. He didn't hesitate, but did tell her that they would have to stop by Jackson, Mississippi on the way to Texas. He was entered in the roping there. Cassie drove to the nearest airport, which was in Tennessee, and picked up Fred. They loaded up and left Alabama.

"We drove to Jackson, Mississippi. It was pretty funny when we pulled into the rodeo grounds in a U-Haul truck towing a pickup behind. The cowboys really gave Fred a hard time."

Fred and Cassie began dating seriously in 1998. Things were going well. She attended the National Finals Rodeo in Las Vegas with him.

"The first few days in Vegas were fine, but after that Fred seemed to forget that I was there," Cassie said. "I didn't know anyone, and no one seemed interested in getting acquainted. Then there was all these cute young things following Fred around. It was hard to deal with. I didn't want to put pressure on Fred with our relationship while he was there to compete. I flew back to Texas for a couple of days. Then I decided to give it another shot and went back to Vegas."

After the competition, Cassie and Fred returned home to Texas. They mutually agreed that it might be best for Cassie to return home to California.

"Fred was leaving to go to Mike Johnson's roping in Tulsa, Oklahoma. I arranged for a U-Haul trailer and had stayed up all night packing. I told him goodbye and wished him good luck. After he left, I headed for California. Fred called me and told me that he really didn't want me to leave, but it might be best. We talked everyday.

"I'd been gone about thirty days when he called me and said, 'I realize that I just let the best thing in my life go.' I told him, 'If you want me back, you're going to have to come and get me.' He came to California, met my mom, and I could tell that he had done some soul searching. He was ready to settle down. We were married April 29, 2000 in San Diego. I had the traditional wedding that had always been my dream."

After the wedding, the couple returned to the rodeo circuit. Cassie traveled with Fred, helping him drive, and care for his horses. One of Fred's sponsors made the very finest horse trailer with living quarters in front. Cassie much preferred the trailer to a motel or camper.

When it came time for Savannah to be born, Fred was roping at Cheyenne, Wyoming. Fred won the roping and arrived home in time to take Cassie to the hospital. He saw his wife and daughter safely home then left for a rodeo. It was several weeks before he was home again. Cassie's mom stayed with her and helped with the baby.

"I think Fred was in shock for a month or two. He didn't know what to do with the baby. After she grew a little, he became comfortable holding her and playing with her."

The three Whitfields traveled together often, but there were times when Cassie and Savannah stayed home. Those are the difficult days having a new baby and all the responsibility alone. Fred missed some important things, like Savannah standing alone and taking her first steps.

By the time Savannah started preschool at three, Cassie was pregnant with Sydney. The girls saw their Dad between rodeos and traveled with him in the summer.

Although life could be lonely at times, Cassie had plenty to keep her busy. She took care of maintenance at the place and managed the paper work. Fred usually had a friend or relative feed the animals for him, but sometimes Cassie did those chores, too.

"Fred doesn't want me to have to worry about the barn or animals. His main concern is that I take care of the girls and the house."

When they first married, an agent took care of Fred's professional schedule. Then Cassie took over as his manager, updating his website, working with sponsors, arranging autograph sessions, booking public appearances, sending in entries, and making travel arrangements. Fred sometimes traveled over 100,000 miles each year to make approximately 100 rodeos. He flew sometimes, but mostly he drove. Sometimes a friend would haul Fred's horse, if Fred flew to a rodeo. There were even times when he would mount someone else's horse.

All the travel and hard work have paid off for Fred. He joined the PRCA in 1990 and won Rookie of the Year. Fred won his first Calf Roping World Championship in 1991, then again in 1995 and 1996. He began team roping as well as calf roping, and was the first African American to win the prestigious All Around Championship in 1999. In 2003 Fred was inducted into the Texas Hall of Fame in Fort Worth. Also in 2003 he became the third cowboy in history to surpass two million dollars in winnings. In 2004 Fred was inducted into the Pro Rodeo Hall of Fame in Colorado Springs, Colorado. In 2005 he was inducted into the Cheyenne Frontier Days Hall of Fame.

Despite her busy schedule and full life, Cassie never lost the need to participate in sports. Over the years she has exercised, practiced yoga, and jogged. When she reached her thirty-fourth birthday, she thought it was time to do something for herself. She heard of an organization that sponsored marathons to raise money for the Leukemia and Lymphoma Society (LLS). She knew that was what she wanted to do. Cassie ran her first marathon June 4, 2006 in San Diego, California.

"I didn't know how hard this was going to be. Most of the time I run after I take the girls to school. That means running by myself at nine o'clock in the morning. It was 90 degrees the other morning. I about died. Thank heavens Fred rode alongside me on his bicycle. I was surprised that he went with me because usually when he's home he's practicing, grooming his horses, or working on tack. He said that he wanted to spend some time with me. That made me feel good."

Cassie trained with a group Saturday mornings. Fred's mother stayed Friday night with Savannah and Sydney so that Cassie could get up at 4:00 a.m. to run. Training with a group helped a great deal and was more fun than running alone.

She never backed away from obstacles and knew about hard work. Her main objective in life was to be a good wife and mother.

"These are my girls and my responsibility," Cassie said. "Fred is a big help when he's home or when we travel with him. He is gone most of the time, but I realize that he is at the peak of his career right now. There may come a time when he has to slow down and do something else. At present he's at the top of his game and I'm standing beside him."

Cassie Loegel crowned 1994 Miss Rodeo Lakeside in Lakeside, California. Left to right: Kandis Ewing, Cassie Loegel, and Karen Ranswieler.

Cassie Loegel performing her duties as Rodeo Queen in 1994.

Cassie Whitfield with daughter Savannah and Cassie's mother in Las Vegas.

Fred and Cassie Whitfield in the living quarters section
of their horse trailer.

Clockwise from top: Fred, Savannah, Sydney, and Cassie Whitfield at the MGM Grand Hotel in Las Vegas, Nevada during the 2005 National Finals Rodeo.

APPENDIX

APPENDIX:
PRCA Events

Below are the rules with accompanying photographs of the PRCA (Professional Rodeo Cowboys' Association) events.

CALF ROPING:

In calf roping, the cowboy must carry two ropes if he intends to use two loops. After throwing the rope around the calf's neck, the cowboy must dismount and move down the rope. He then throws the calf by hand, crossing and tying any three feet. If the calf is down when he reaches it, the cowboy must allow the calf to stand before throwing it. If the cowboy's hand is on the calf when it falls, the calf is considered thrown by hand. The tie must hold for six seconds, after the roper calls for time and slacks the rope.

STEER ROPING:

In steer roping, the rider throws the rope around the steer and turns away his horse, causing the steer to fall. The roper dismounts and ties three of the steer's feet. If the steer stays tied for six seconds, it is a qualified run.

STEER WRESTLING:

In steer wrestling, the steer must be caught from the horse. If the steer gets loose, the cowboy may take no more than one step to catch him. The steer will be considered down only when it is lying flat on its side with all four feet and the head straight.

TEAM ROPING:

In team roping, ropes are loose from the saddle horns. After making the catch, the ropers must take a wrap around the horn. Time is taken when both ropes are tight and both horses are facing the steer. There are strict rules defining a fair head catch. The rope must be around the horns, the neck, or one horn and neck. There is a five-second fine for a head catch (with or without a figure-8), that also catches a front foot. There is also a five-second fine for catching only one hind foot.

BARREL RACING:

Barrel racing is a timed event. The contestant is allowed a running start. The clock shall start as soon as the horse's nose reaches the starting line and it will stop when the horse's nose crosses the finish line. The starting and finishing lines are the same. The contestant will ride in a cloverleaf pattern, starting either to left or right. A five-second penalty will be added to time for each barrel knocked over during the ride. Disqualification will come if the designated pattern is broken.

BAREBACK BRONC RIDING:

In bareback riding, a one-hand rigging is to be used. To qualify, the rider must have spurs over the break of the shoulders when the horse's front feet touch the ground. Horses will be ridden for eight seconds. The rider cannot touch the horse with his free hand.

SADDLE BRONC RIDING:

In saddle bronc riding, the riding rein and the cowboy's hand must be on the same side. The ride is to be eight seconds. To qualify, the rider must have his spurs over the break of the bronc's shoulders and must be touching the horse when its front feet hit the ground on the first jump out of the chute. The rider will be disqualified for any of the following: being bucked off; changing hands on the rein; losing the stirrup; or touching the animal or saddle or rein with the free hand.

BULL RIDING:

Bull riding is to be done with one hand and a loose rope with a bell attached. The bull will be ridden for eight seconds. The rider will be disqualified for being bucked off or for touching the animal with the free hand.

ABOUT
THE
AUTHOR

Judy Goodspeed

Judy Goodspeed is the daughter of Buck Goodspeed, professional steer roper and Cowboy Hall of Fame honoree, and Decie Goodspeed, whose life story is included in this book. She spent much of her childhood at the practice arena or attending rodeos with her dad.

Judy is a graduate of Wetumka High School in Wetumka, Oklahoma and of East Central State College in Ada, Oklahoma. She was a Junior High School teacher and coach for thirty years.

After retiring from teaching, she began writing. She has had articles published in *Outdoor Oklahoma, Good Old Days*, and *The Ketchpen* (a publication of the Rodeo Historical Society). She was a contributing writer for the *Wewoka Times* and published articles in the *Holdenville Tribune*. She is the author of the children's picture books *Perky Turkey's Perfect Plan, Perky Turkey Finds a Friend*, and *Saddle Up*.

Judy is a member of the Professional and Amateur Writers Society (PAWS) and the Oklahoma Writers Federation, Inc. (OWFI). She lives on a farm in rural Oklahoma.

INDEX

INDEX

Pages with photographs are in italics.

www.ingramcontent.com/pod-product-compliance
Lightning Source LLC
Chambersburg PA
CBHW032105280326
41933CB00009B/761